Drawing Faeries

A Believer's Guide

W9-AZR-594

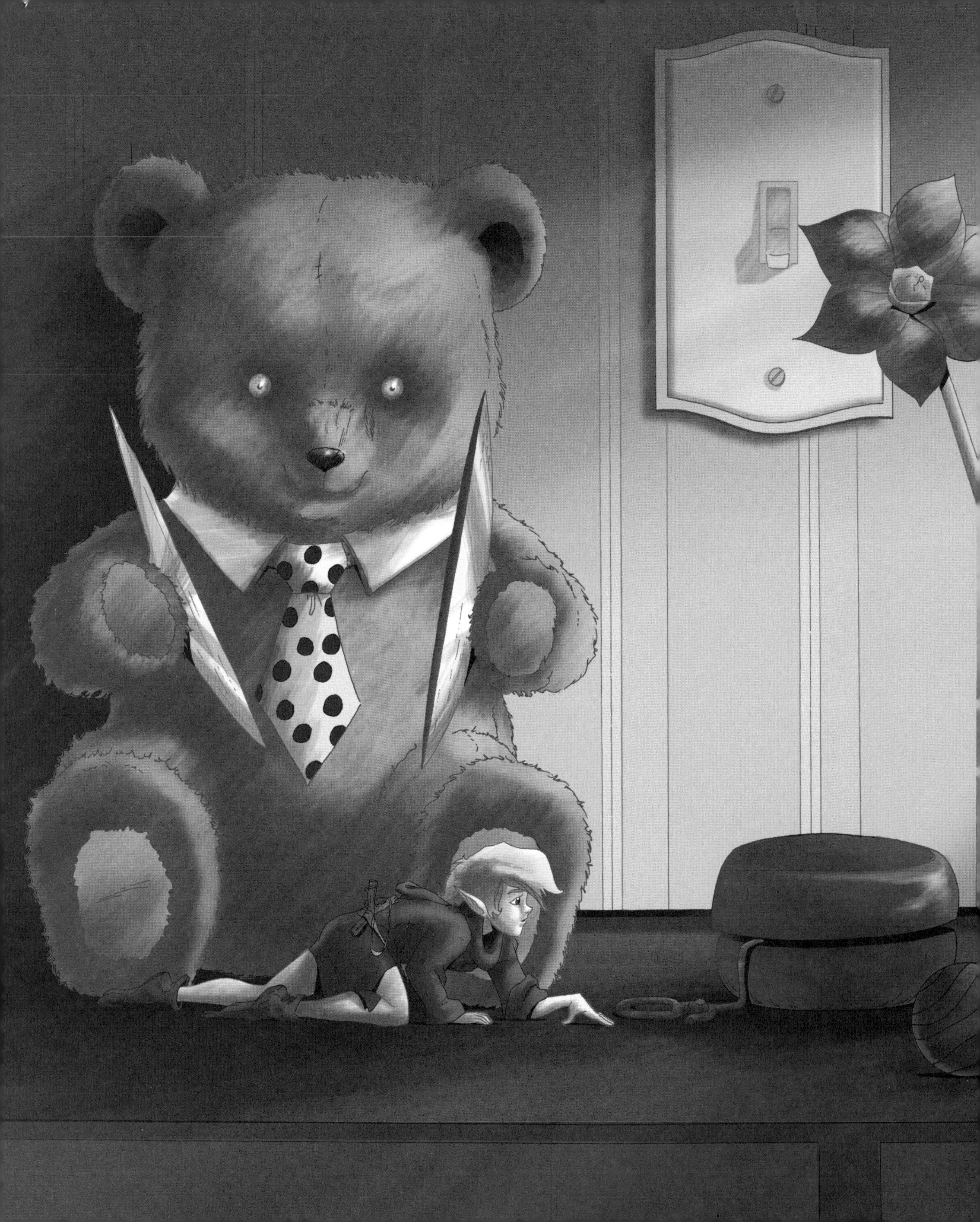

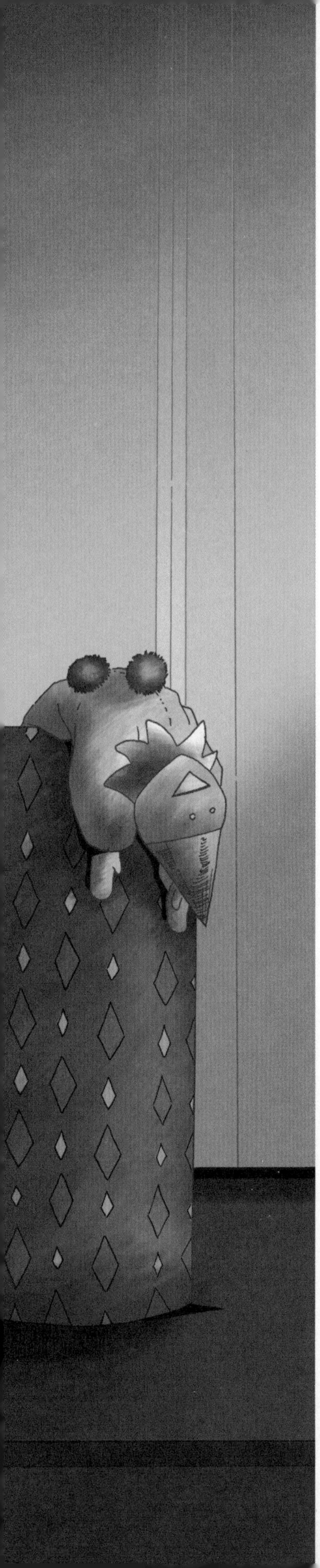

Drawing Faeries

A Believer's Guide

CHRISTOPHER
HART

Watson-Guptill Publications/New York

For Isabella and Francesca, my
inspirations, my muses, my angels.
And for Maria, forever.

Senior Acquisitions Editor: Candace Raney
Editor: Anne McNamara
Contributing Editor: Alisa Palazzo
Designer: Derek Bacchus
Graphic Production: Ellen Greene
Color by MADA Design, Inc.

Copyright © 2004 by Christopher Hart

First published in 2004 by Watson-Guptill Publications,
a division of VNU Business Media, Inc.,
770 Broadway, New York, N. Y. 10003
www.watsonguptill.com

All rights reserved. No part of this publication may be
reproduced or used in any form or by any means—
graphic, electronic, or mechanical, including photocopying,
recording, taping, or information storage-and-retrieval
systems—without written permission from the publisher.

Library of Congress Cataloging-in-Publication Data

Hart, Christopher.
  Drawing faeries : a believer's guide / by Christopher Hart.
     p. cm.
ISBN 0-8230-1403-7 (pb)
1. Fairies in art. 2. Drawing—Technique. I. Title.
NC825.F22H37 2004
743'.8939821—dc22

Manufactured in Singapore

First printing, 2004

1 2 3 4 5 6 7 8 / 11 10 09 08 07 06 05 04

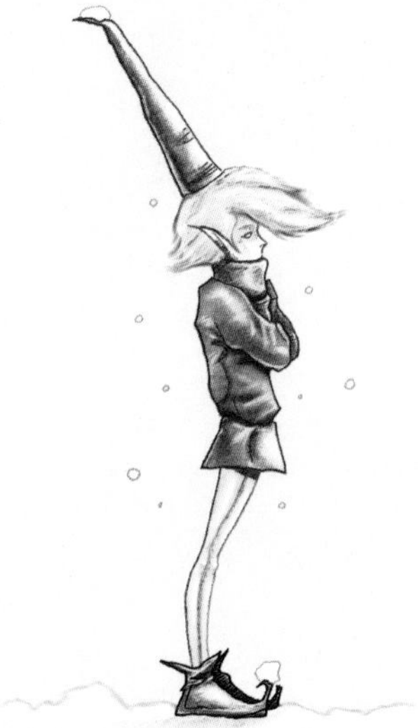

Table of Contents

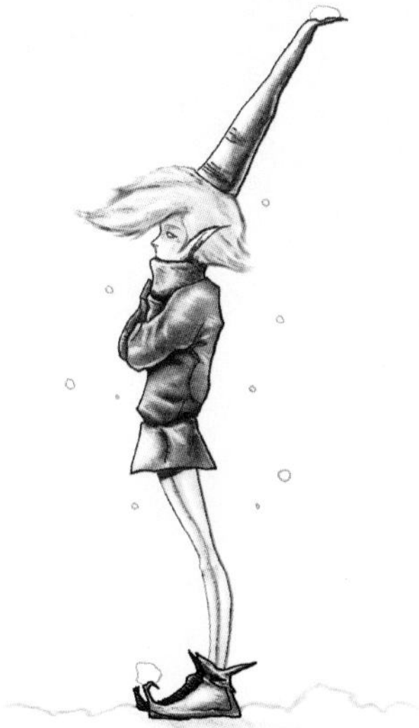

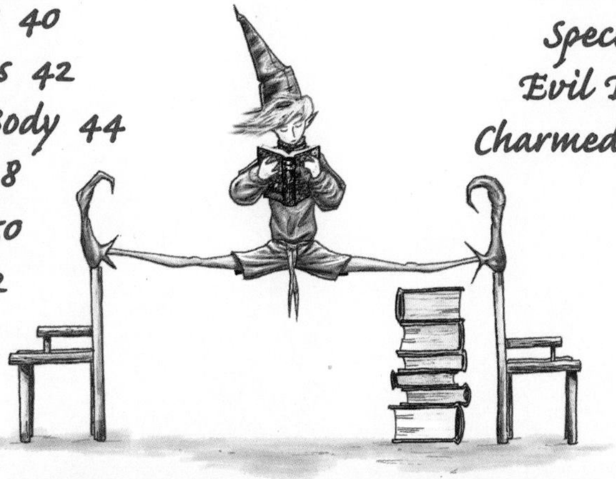

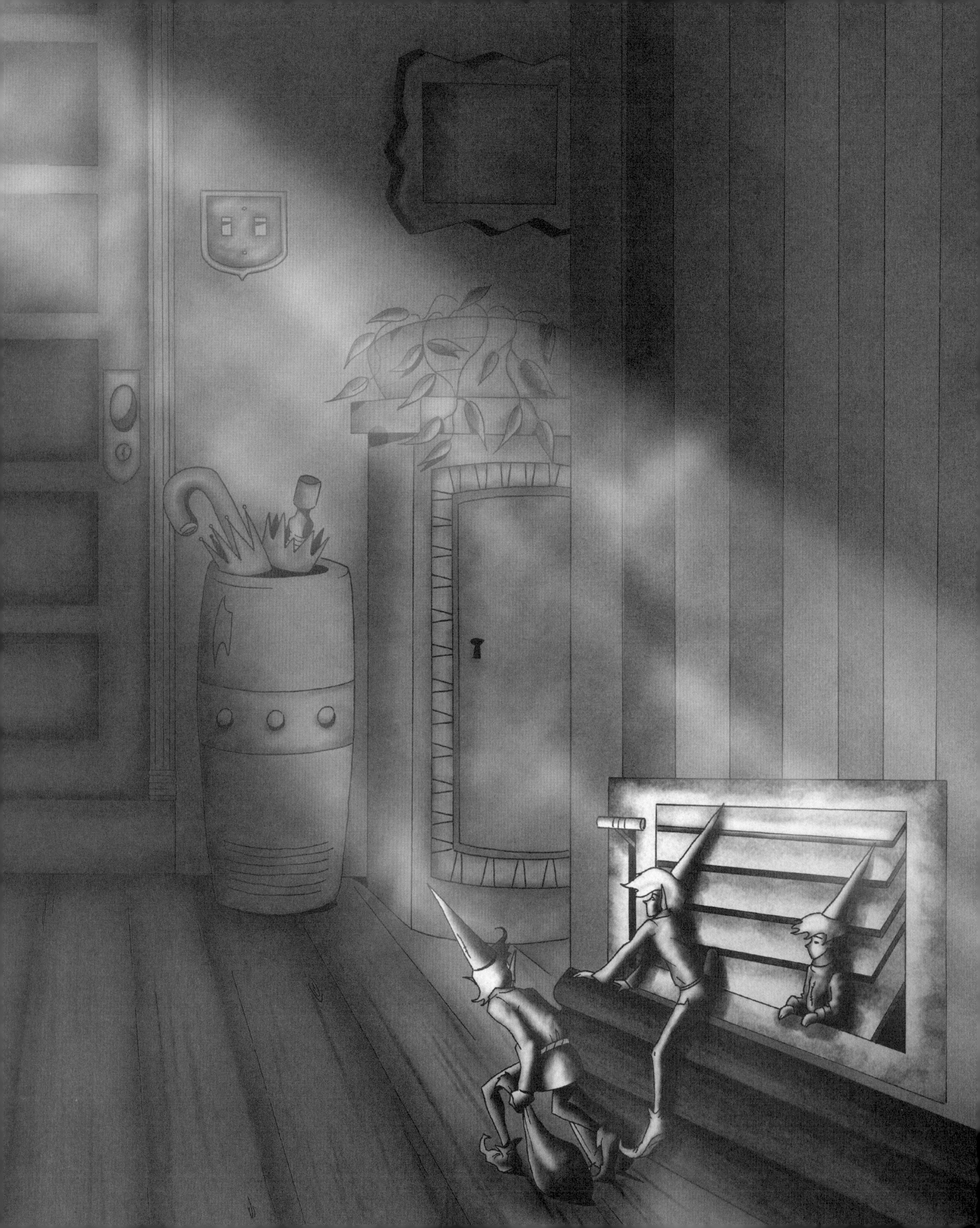

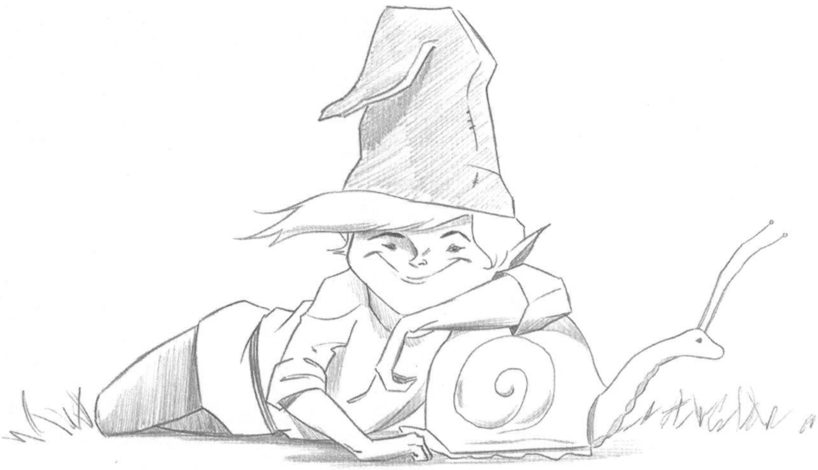

Introduction

So often, as artists, we dive into the act of drawing without first immersing ourselves in that dreamlike state from which our images are borrowed. That state of mind is never more necessary than when drawing faeries. Some say these creatures exist; others say they are creations of a fertile imagination. I won't take sides on this contentious issue. However, in order to draw faeries, you must first put yourself into the mind-set of one who believes—it is the only way to bring that magic to life.

That is why I have approached this book in a manner different from any of my previous works. As inspiration is the most important element in an artist's mind, I begin by weaving a magical tale to spark the imagination. I encourage you to suspend your disbelief and follow my thoughts as they wander into a world of enchantment and wonder. Once there, I will introduce you to a full cast of faerie characters in all manners of dress and circumstance. You will find many suggestions on how to draw these delightful creatures, as well as tips on making lands where your faeries can roam.

Faeries are wonderful subjects to draw; and the creative possibilities are endless. So, we begin with the tale of the little faerie that entered my home one snowy night, many years ago. Some say it is only a tale. Others say it is true. I shall let you decide for yourselves.

C. Hart

A Faerie Tale

I was sitting at my drawing desk, gazing out the window at the blizzard swirling around outdoors and thinking of nothing. My pen had refused to emit so much as an inspired line. There were no happy accidents on paper that could be turned into a successful drawing. My muse had abandoned me, and I feared that this time it was gone for good. My thoughts drifted, and I began to reminisce upon some of my earliest sources of inspiration...

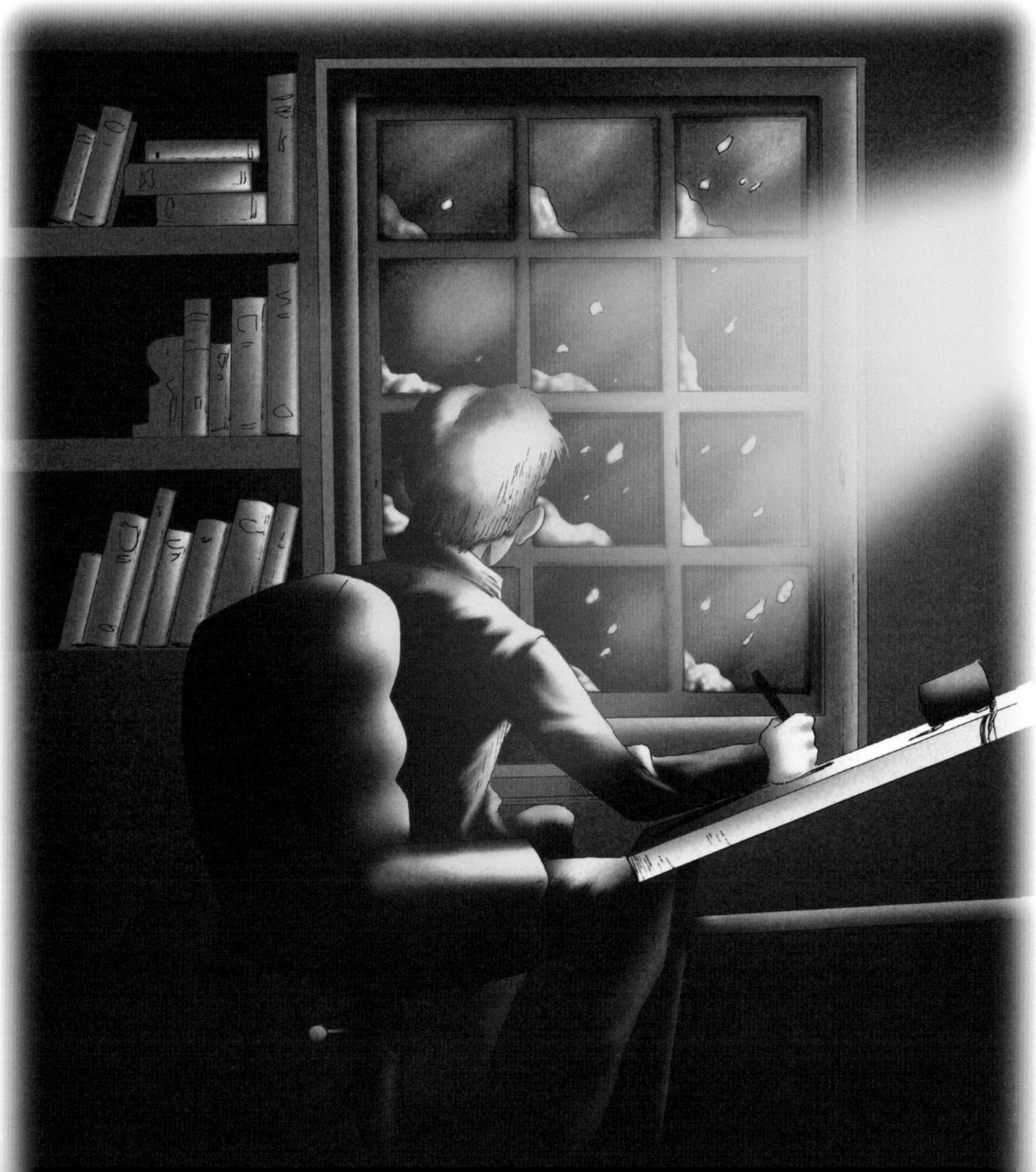

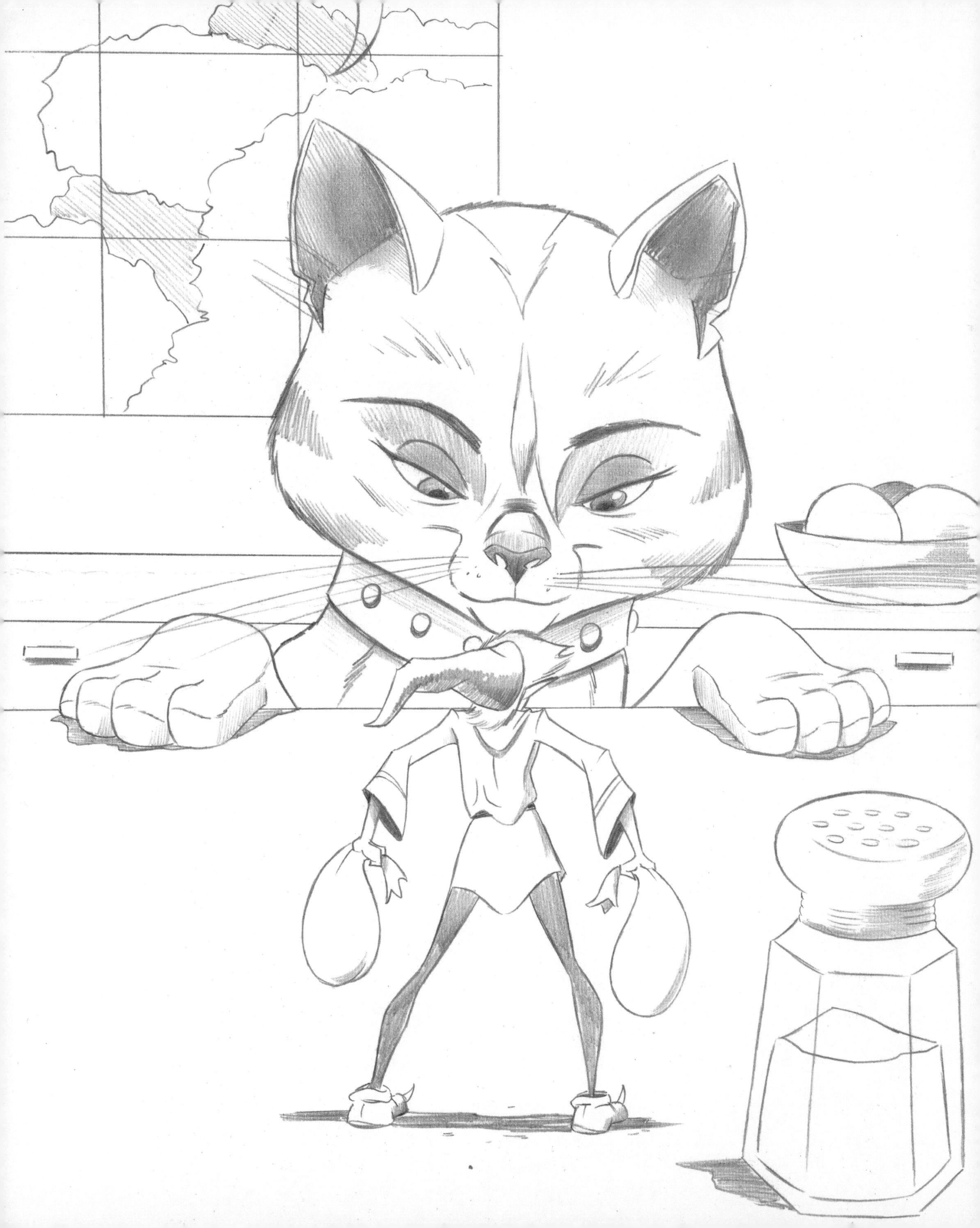

I was a boy of nine, growing up in New England. It was a snowy winter night, much like this one, and I was bundled up in a goose down comforter, fast asleep in a delicious slumber…when it happened. There was a bump, then a crash. I jumped. The family cat had caught something in my room. It was the size of a mouse, no, even smaller, perhaps only slightly bigger than an acorn. As I came forward for a closer inspection, I saw something astonishing. It was a tiny man with pointed ears, an upturned nose, and terrified little eyes. In a small voice, he told me he was on a serious mission and begged me not to let the cat eat him. I removed the little fellow from the reluctant cat's mouth and listened as he explained the desperate need that brought him to my home…

He said his name was Rollo Häavalhorn, and that he was a faerie, one of many in a society of nature's tiniest beings. He explained that faeries are especially fond of milk, and often milk the cows as they graze the fields. But with the unseasonably hard winter, and snowdrifts piling up outdoors, the faeries had to resort to stealing milk from humans.

But his own hunger was the least of his concerns. He had a baby daughter, a faerie baby, and there was simply no food left in his village. I soon learned that although faeries are healthy, long-lived folk, their first year of life is extremely precarious, due to their diminutive size.

There was fear in his eyes, such that I did not doubt the urgency of his cause.

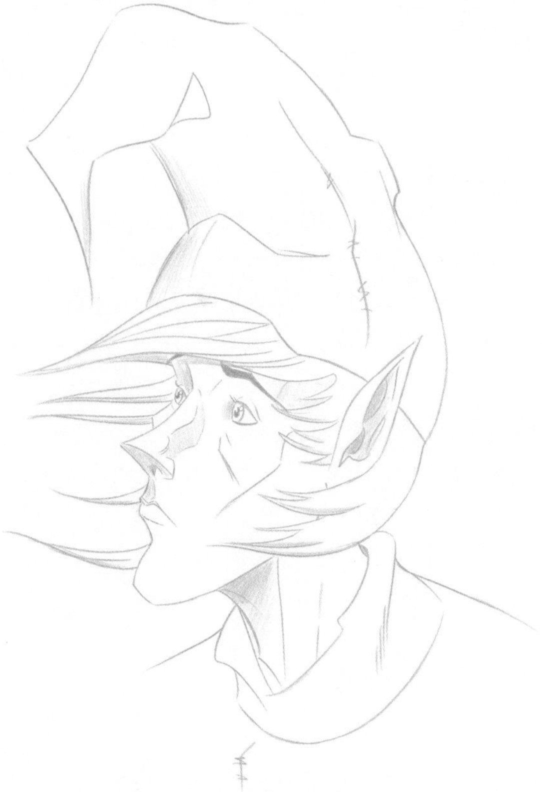

He said he chose my house because it did not have a cat. Obviously, it was one of his poorer choices. We crept into the kitchen together and stuffed his bags to the brim.

I wanted to go with him—I just had to see more of these fantastic creatures. But he said that it was against the rules, forbidden by *The Great Book of Faerie,* the laws and traditions for all faerie life. Disappointed, I was about to hand him the sacks of food when I noticed that his leg had been badly hurt in the scuffle with the cat. He was in no condition to ferry his parcels through the storm.

I again pressed him to accept my help. Though he tried, his mind could not argue with my logic, and he reluctantly accepted my offer. In a grave voice, he instructed me to place both of my hands over my heart, and to repeat a solemn oath, an oath that I have kept to this day, which prevents me from revealing the exact location of the faerie kingdom.

I quickly stuffed my little friend into my pants pocket, put on my boots and jacket, and ventured forth into the night air. It was a blinding snowstorm. Rollo directed me into the wetlands and over the marshes covered with sheets of ice. After about twenty minutes, I became disoriented, but my little friend never wavered, directing my steps with the precision of a pilot. Deeper through the marsh and into the forest we went.

My eyes burned from the whipping wind and my feet were numb with cold. I wished I had worn that itchy, old sweater my mother always pestered me about. Onward we trudged. After what seemed like hours, my entire body began to tremble with cold and exhaustion. I seriously doubted that I could go any further. Yet, somehow, we pressed on. "Just up ahead!" he would say, "Not much further now!" I lost count, but there were many more "Not much further now's" than I had anticipated. We continued until I couldn't move another inch. I wanted to yell at him—tell him that I had had enough—and I would have, but as I looked up through my snow-covered lashes, I suddenly saw the most glorious sight. It was a village, with scores of them, little people, all playing and working in harmony.

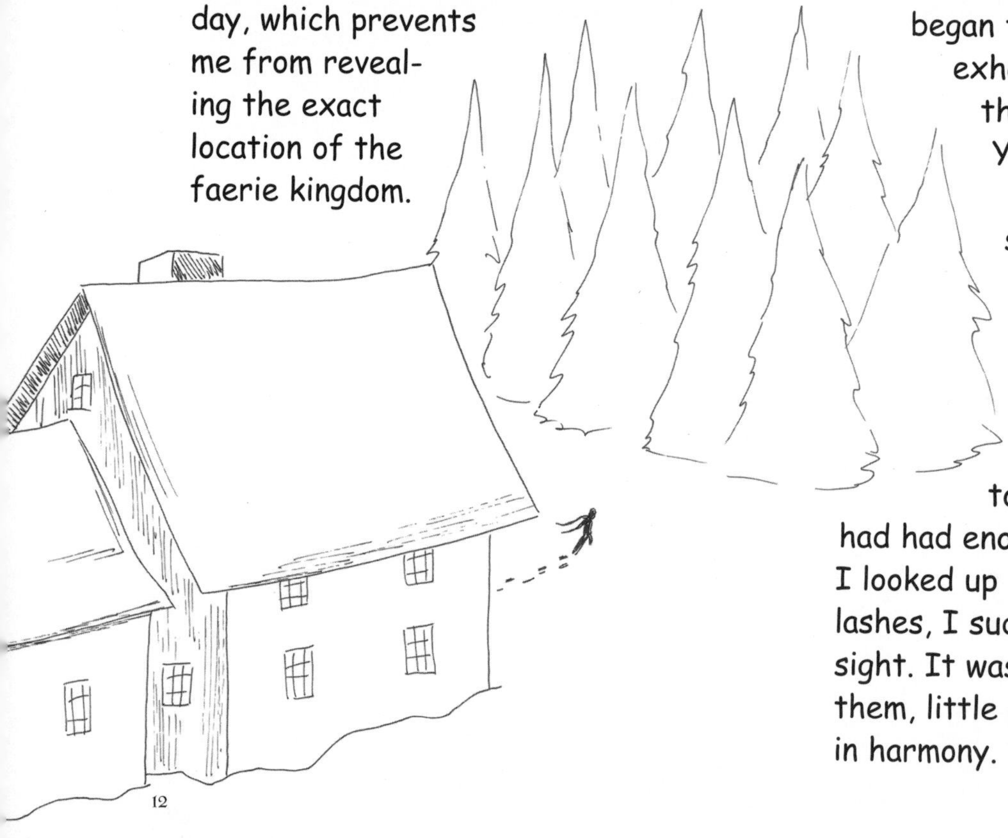

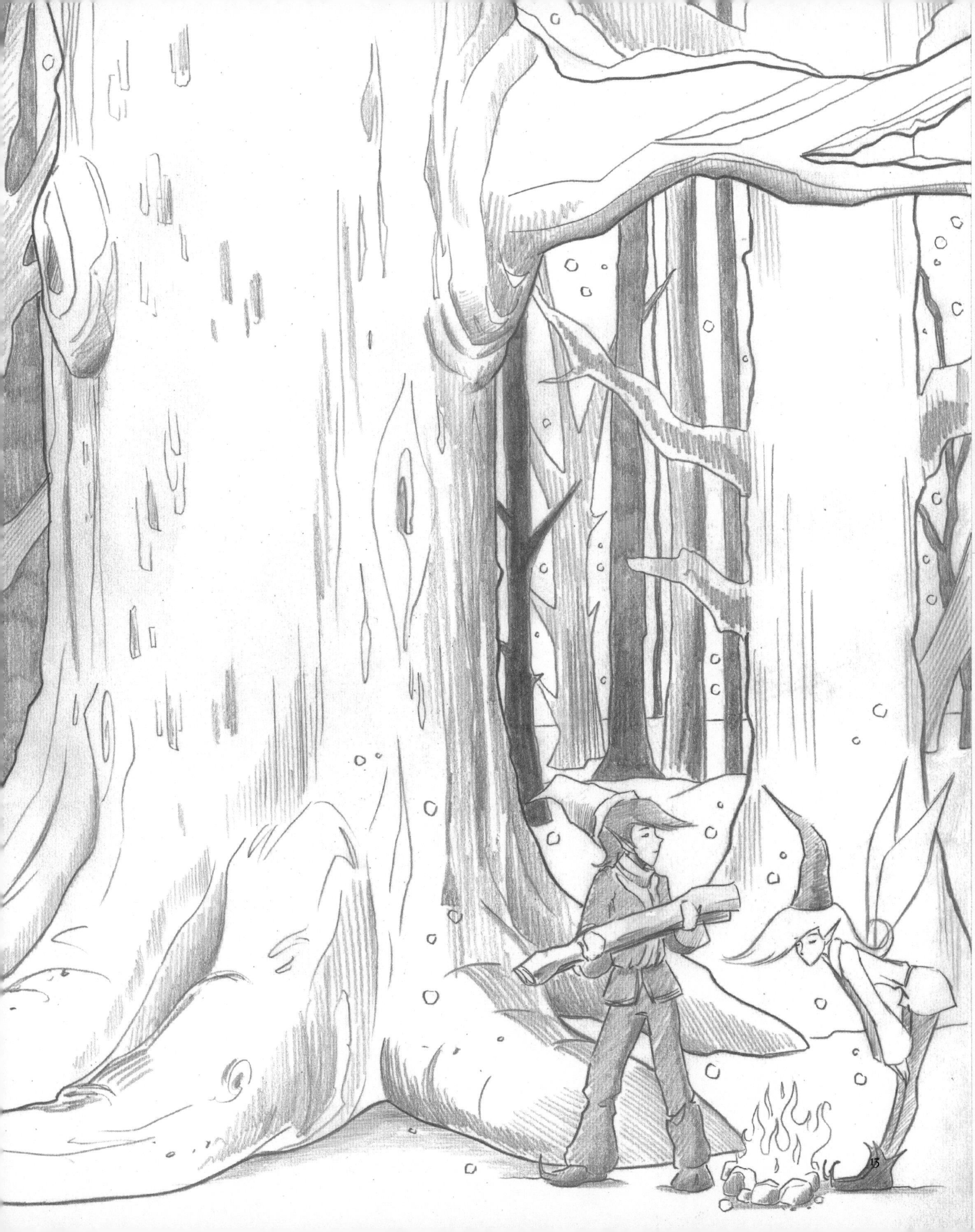

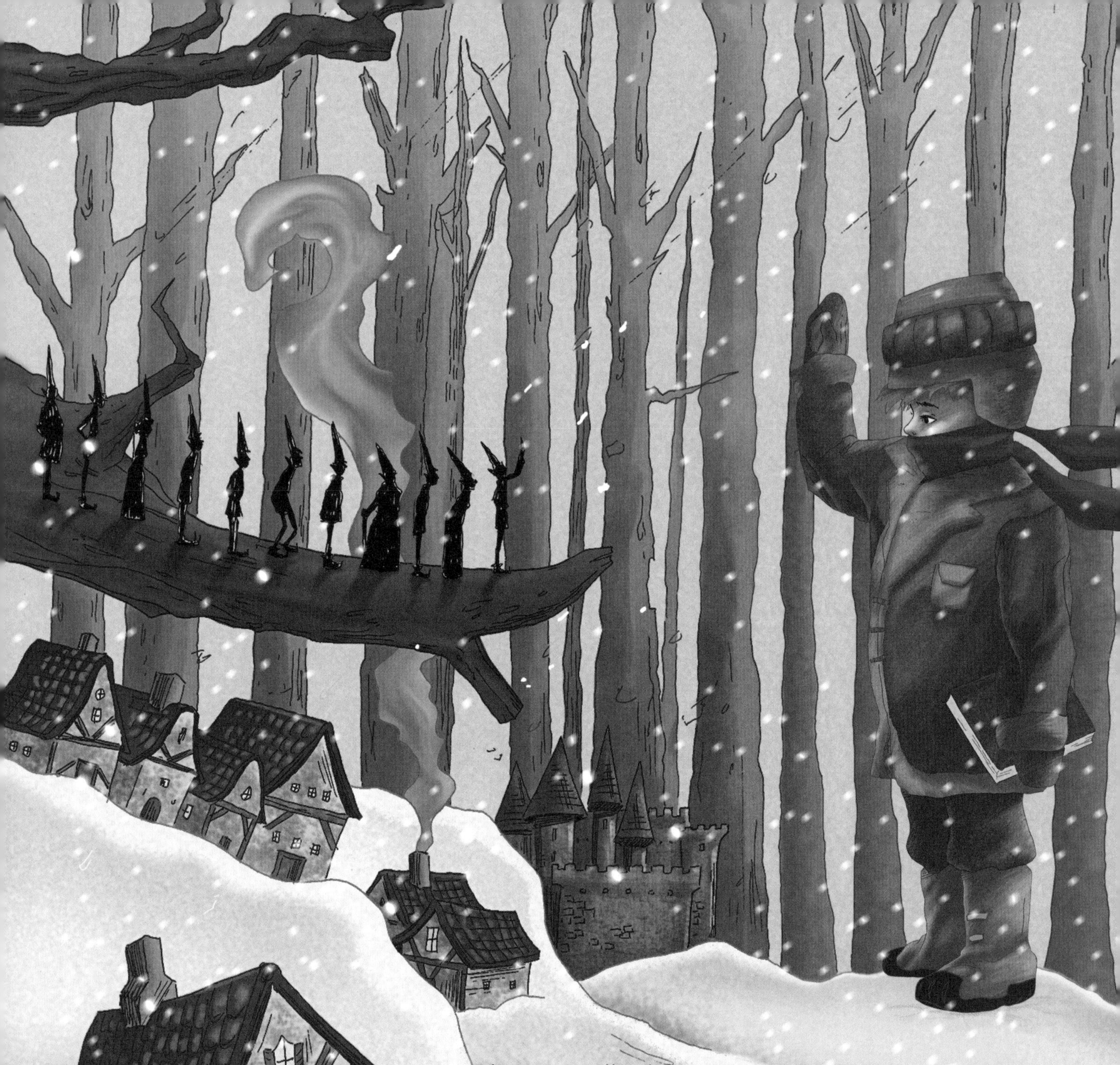

They were all aghast to see me, but Rollo convinced them that I had come as a friend and had taken an oath of secrecy. And besides, I was a child, and therefore, could be trusted, whereas no adult could, regardless of swearing a hundred oaths. Upon his request, I repeated my oath to the Faerie King, using the most solemn face I could muster (which wasn't easy, because my face was still numb). I think I must have repeated the oath to each and every faerie, because my throat was hoarse by the time I got back home.

I visited that tiny village twice more that winter and often over the summer months. I kept my promise and told no one of my secret. I brought the faeries little gifts and became a trusted friend. I sketched the faeries in a book so that I could always remember them.

I drew faeries of all ages and sorts, at work and at play, trying to capture in art all aspects of faerie life. It was at this time that I decided to become an artist. But as children do, I grew older, and my interests turned to other things. There were sports, and girls, and work, and then a career to worry about. I visited the faerie village less and less frequently, and eventually lost all contact with my special little friends. It has been many years since I last thought about them, but tonight, sitting at my desk, with my imagination flatlining for the third month in a row, I knew that somehow, I had to make the journey to the kingdom once more. I had learned their tricks, how they hide from those who do not believe. I knew that this time it would be different, for I was now an adult, and they would not willingly reveal themselves to me; I would not be trusted. But I could, if I were very careful and quiet, observe, and perhaps—just perhaps—gain some of the magic that I had left behind long ago.

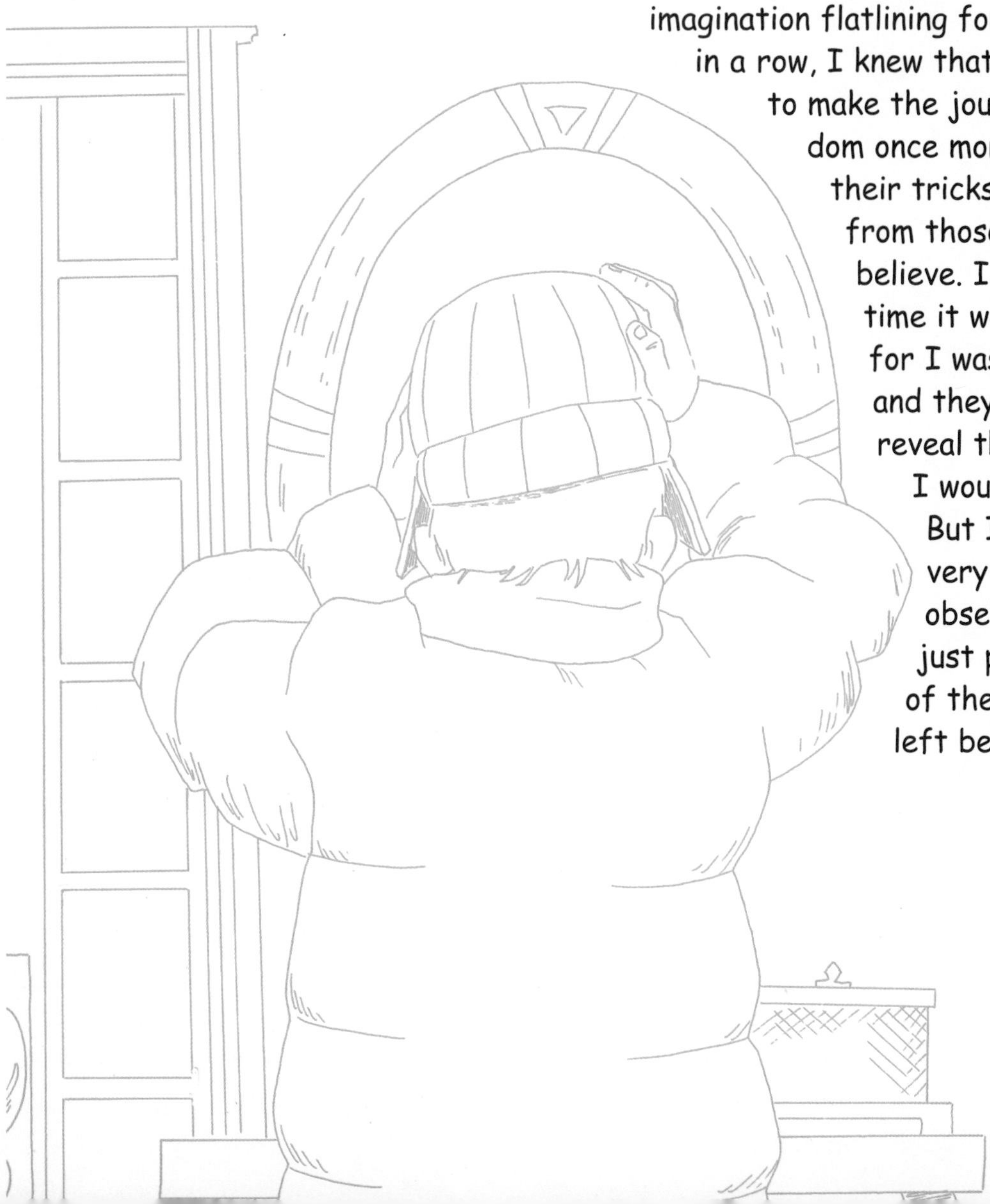

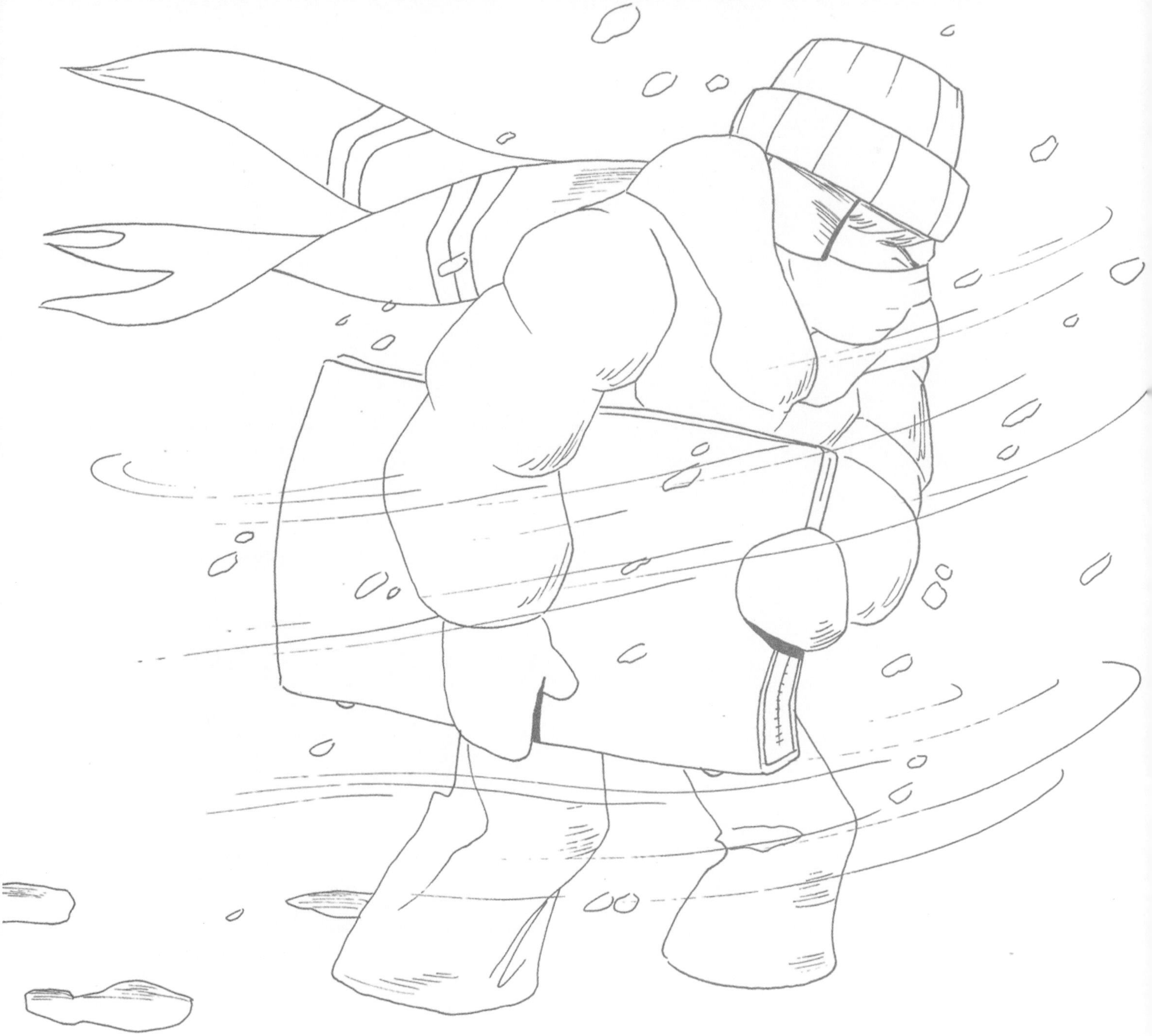

I grabbed my sketchpad, put on my hiking boots, jacket, and cap, and set off into the woods. The journey took every bit as long as I remembered as a child. Unfortunately, wearing a hat did not help, because my ears were now home to a convention of icicles. I continued on, turning left, then right, then up a hill, then down, guided only by my memories.

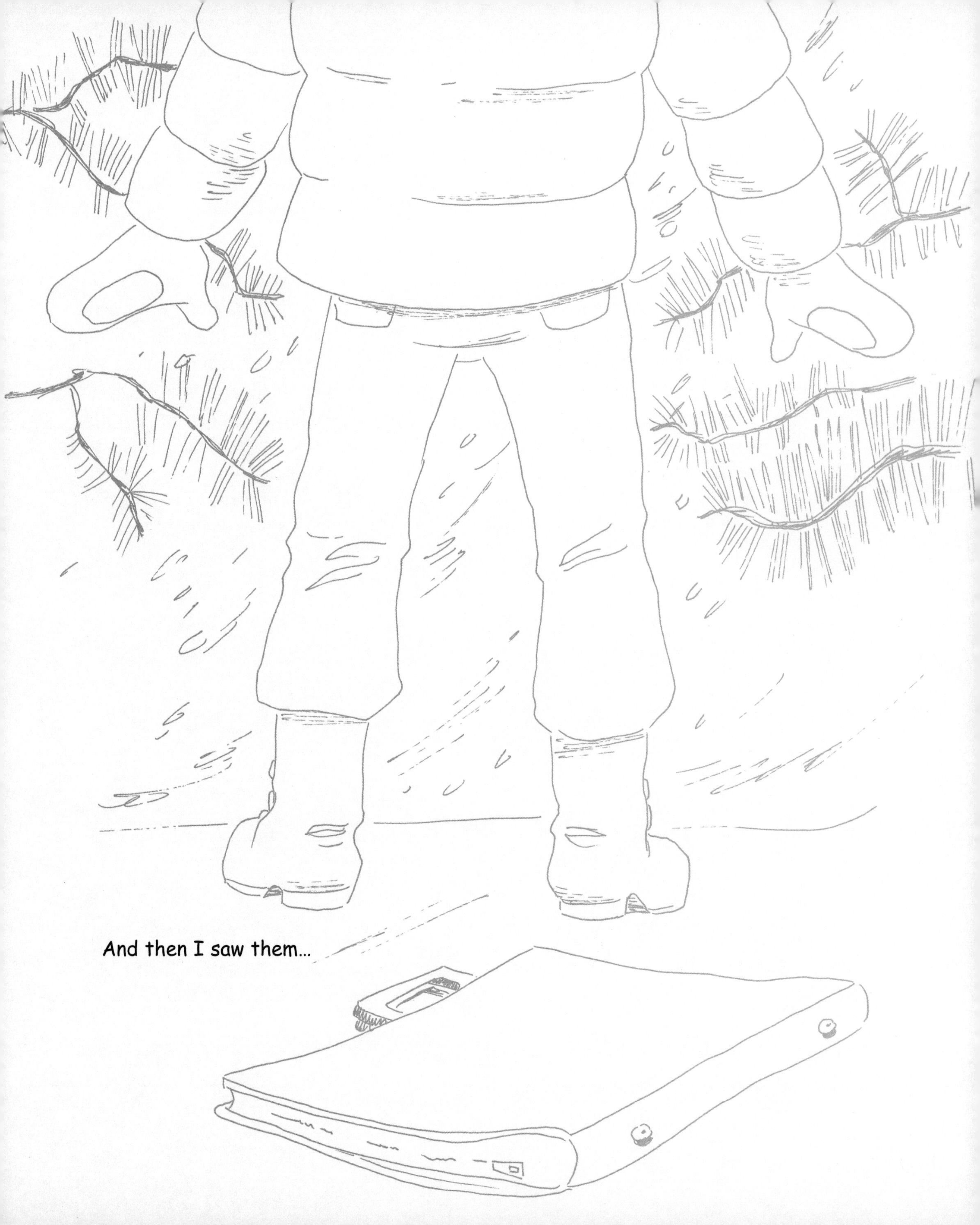
And then I saw them...

I sat back and quietly recorded everything I observed. My pen seemed to flow of its own accord, as drawing after drawing bounded onto the paper. I had found the magic that is still there—the magic that we cannot own, but can only borrow when our hearts and minds are truly open to it.

What you will find here is my sketchpad, filled with drawings and notes from my firsthand observations. My drawings contain step-by-step instructions and details to remind me of exactly how to draw the faeries. It is my hope that you may find them useful, too.

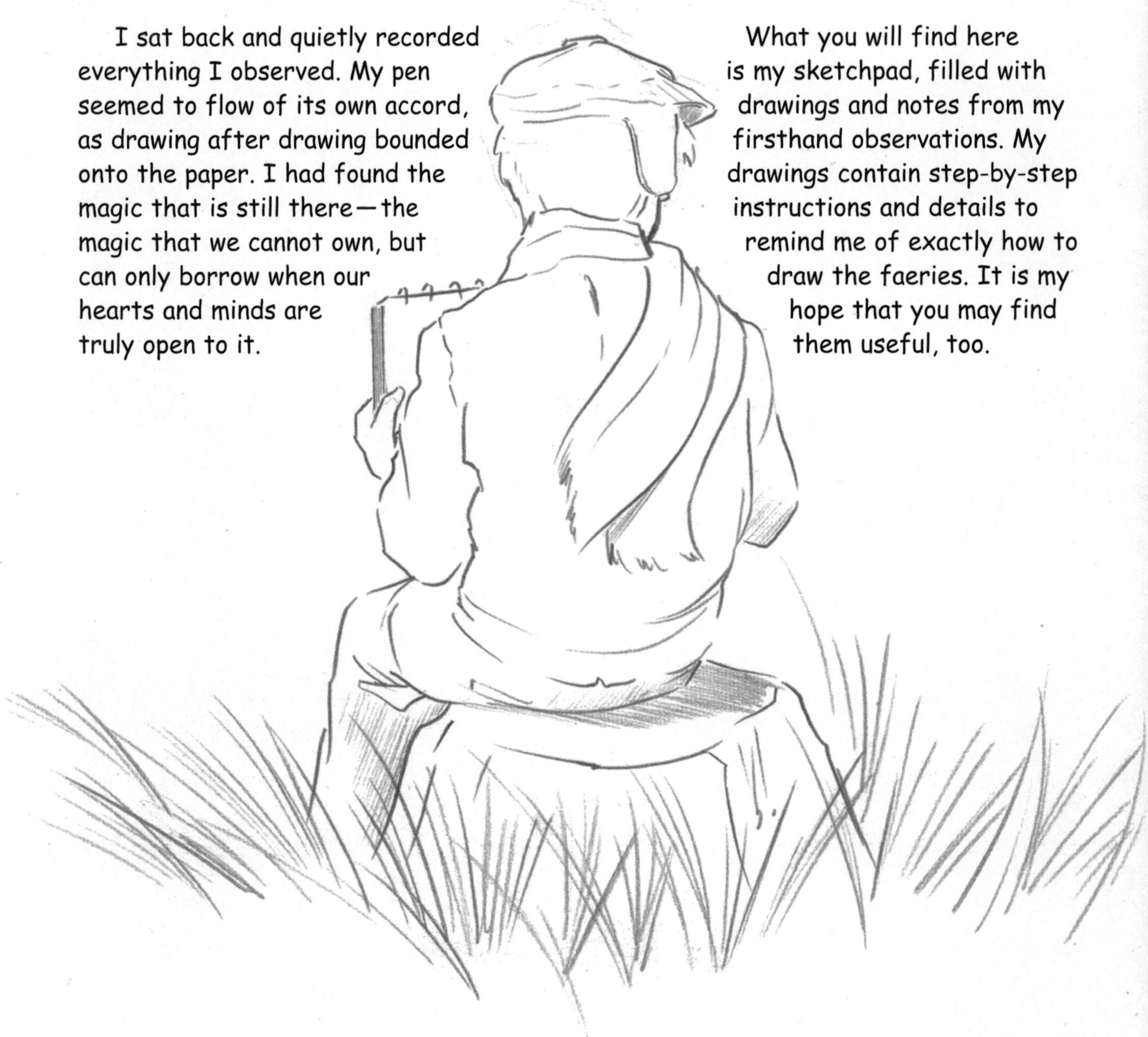

My Faerie Sketchbook

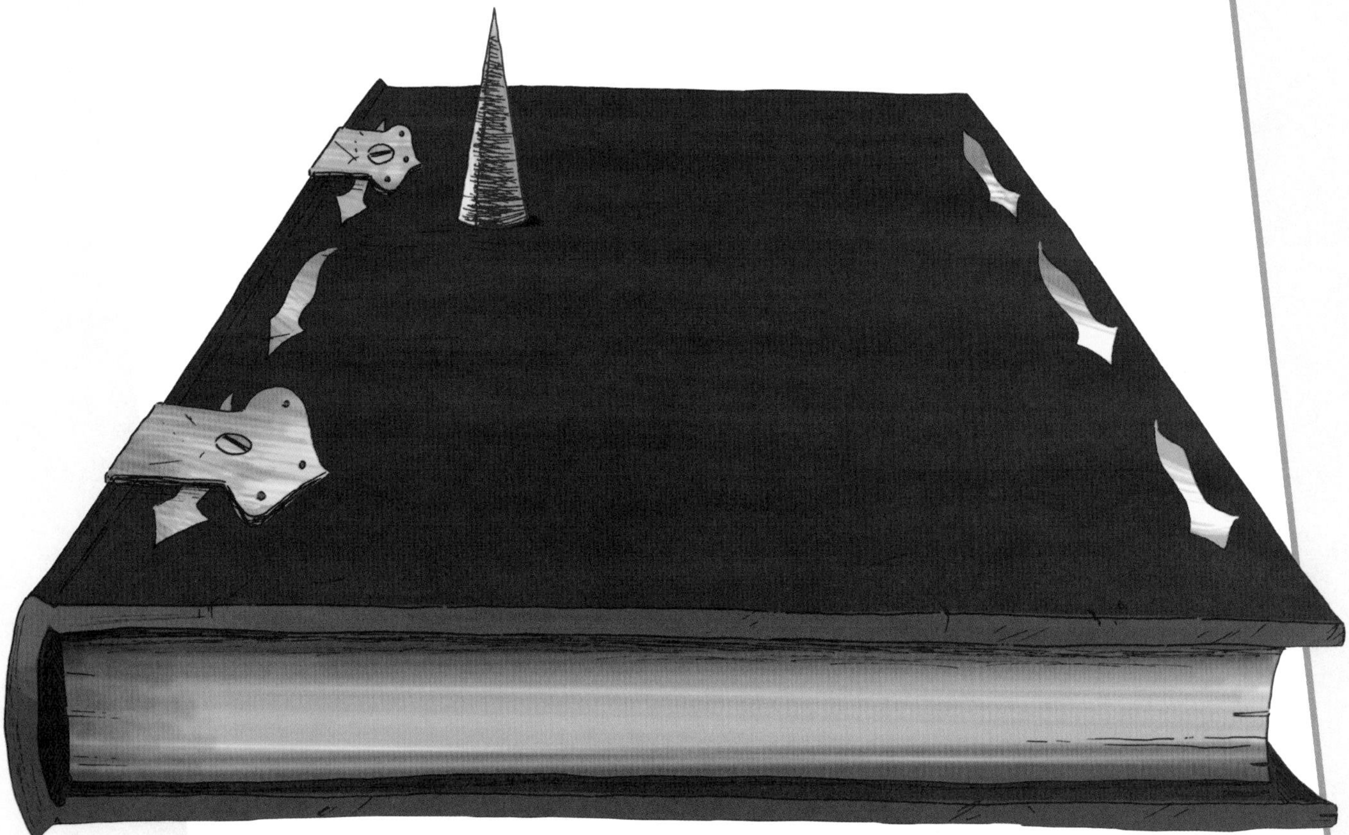

Faerie Faces

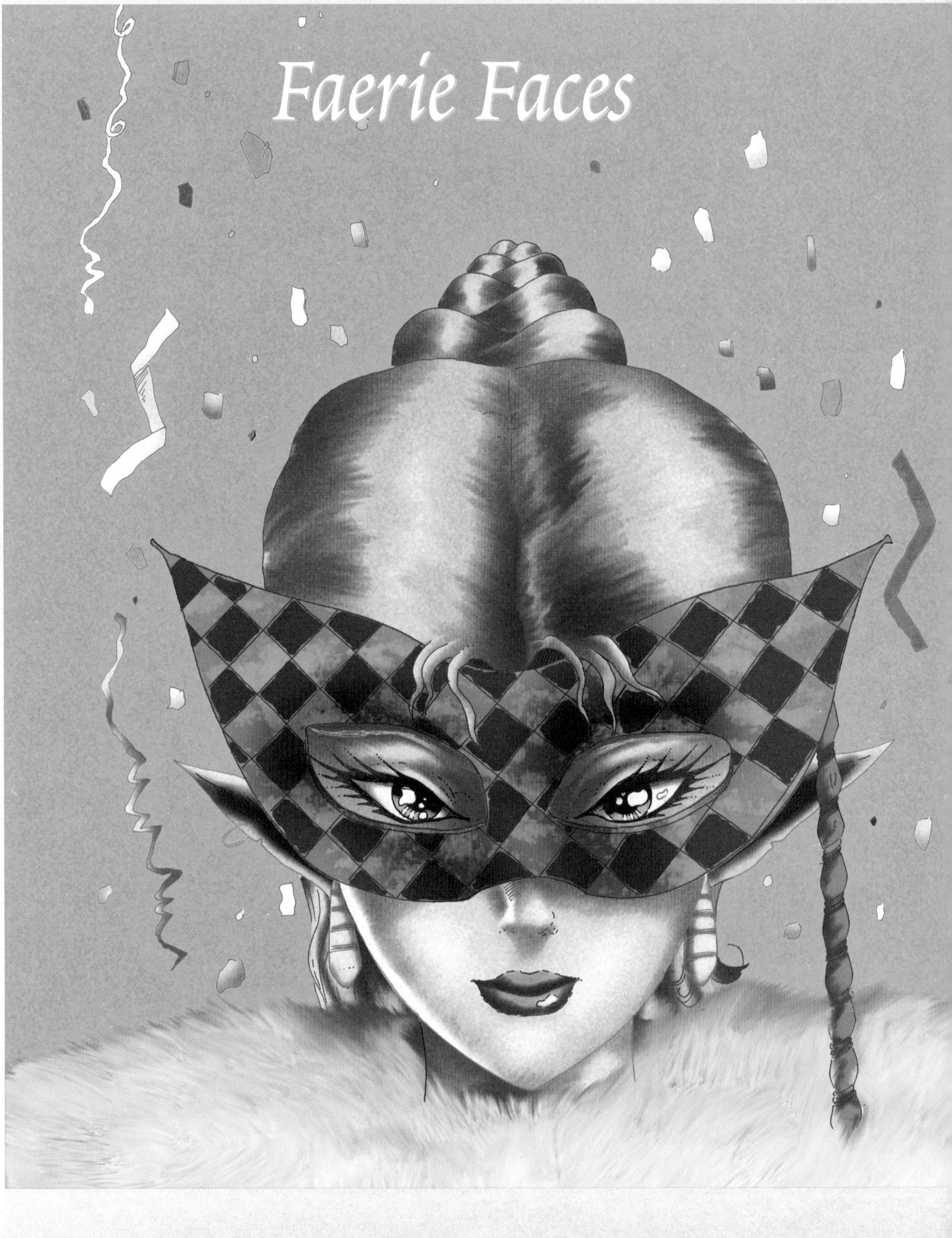

The Features

Of all the subjects I have drawn, faeries are the most intriguing. Their features are quite delicate, and yet the impression they make on humans is profound. I believe it begins with the elegant simplicity of their features.

Faeries' eyes are shaped differently from humans'. They are slightly elongated, lifted at the ends, and pointed at the outer edges. It is not the eyelid that causes this elegant, distinct look, but rather the shape of the eyeball itself.

Human Eye

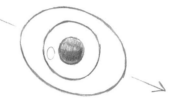

Faerie Eye

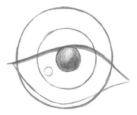

Human Eye (covered)

Faerie Eye (covered)

Whereas the human eyeball is spherical, the faeries' is oval. The eyelid is simply stretched in order to cover the longer surface.

Of all of nature's creatures, faeries have the most expressive eyes. They naturally glisten, even when the surroundings are dim or in shadow. Their eyes often have several shines in them, which may appear in the iris, pupil, or even the whites. They are long lashed and elegant, revealing a remarkable degree of vulnerability and empathy.

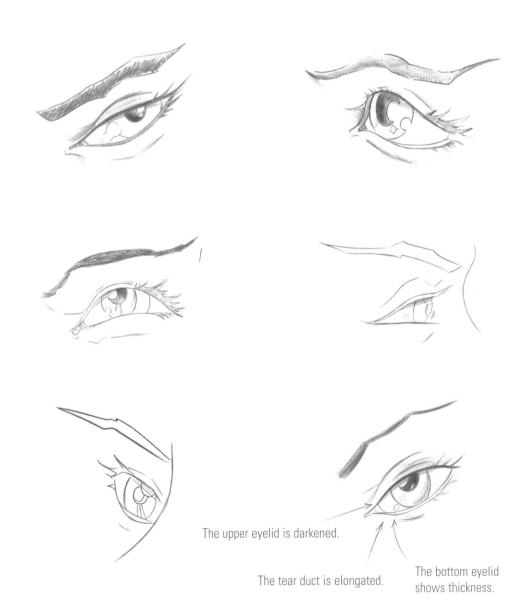

The upper eyelid is darkened.

The tear duct is elongated.

The bottom eyelid shows thickness.

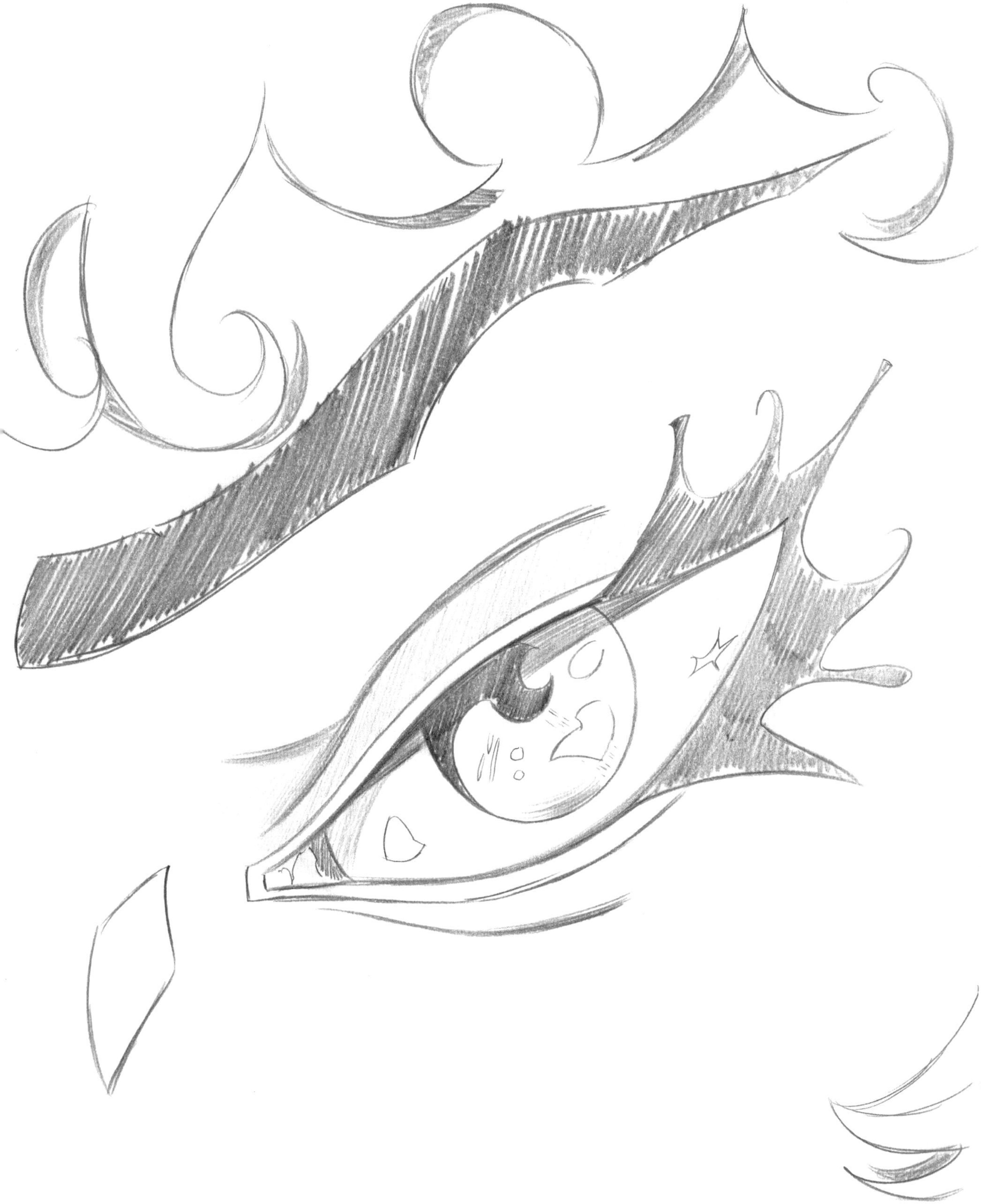

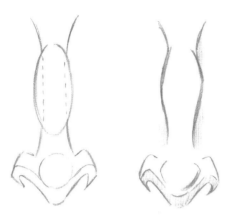

The faerie nose is chiseled and well articulated. Because it is so slender, the bridge of the nose, by contrast, seems to bulge. The nostrils may appear somewhat flared because the tip of the nose is so pointed.

Human Ear versus Faerie Ear

The faerie ear is a finely tuned instrument. It reaches out to capture the faintest sound, giving a faerie ample time to evade detection.

While there are many things that impress me about faerie heads, the one that stands out most in my mind is that their hair is always *windswept*. So fine is their hair that it will catch even the faintest hint of a breeze.

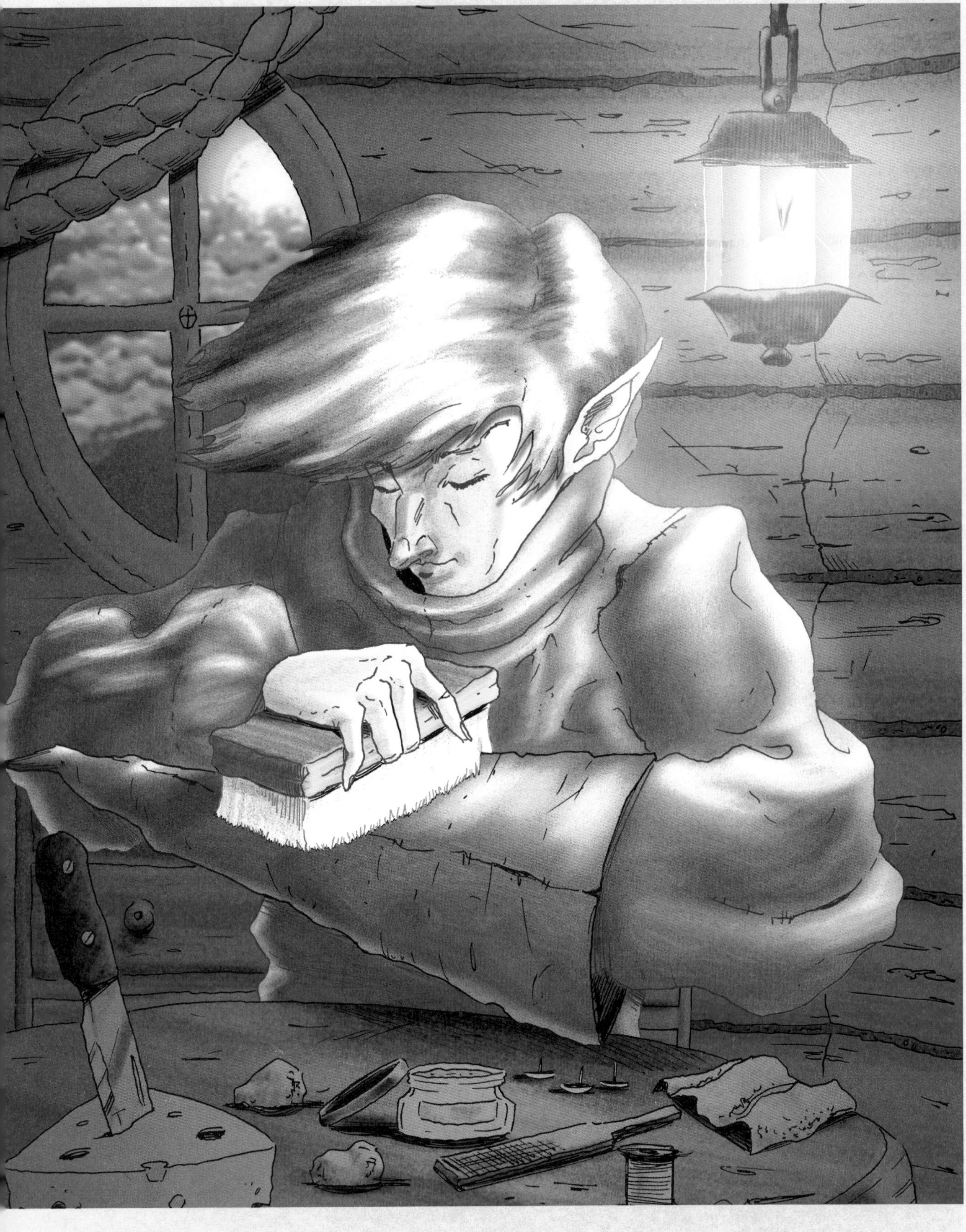

Facial Structure

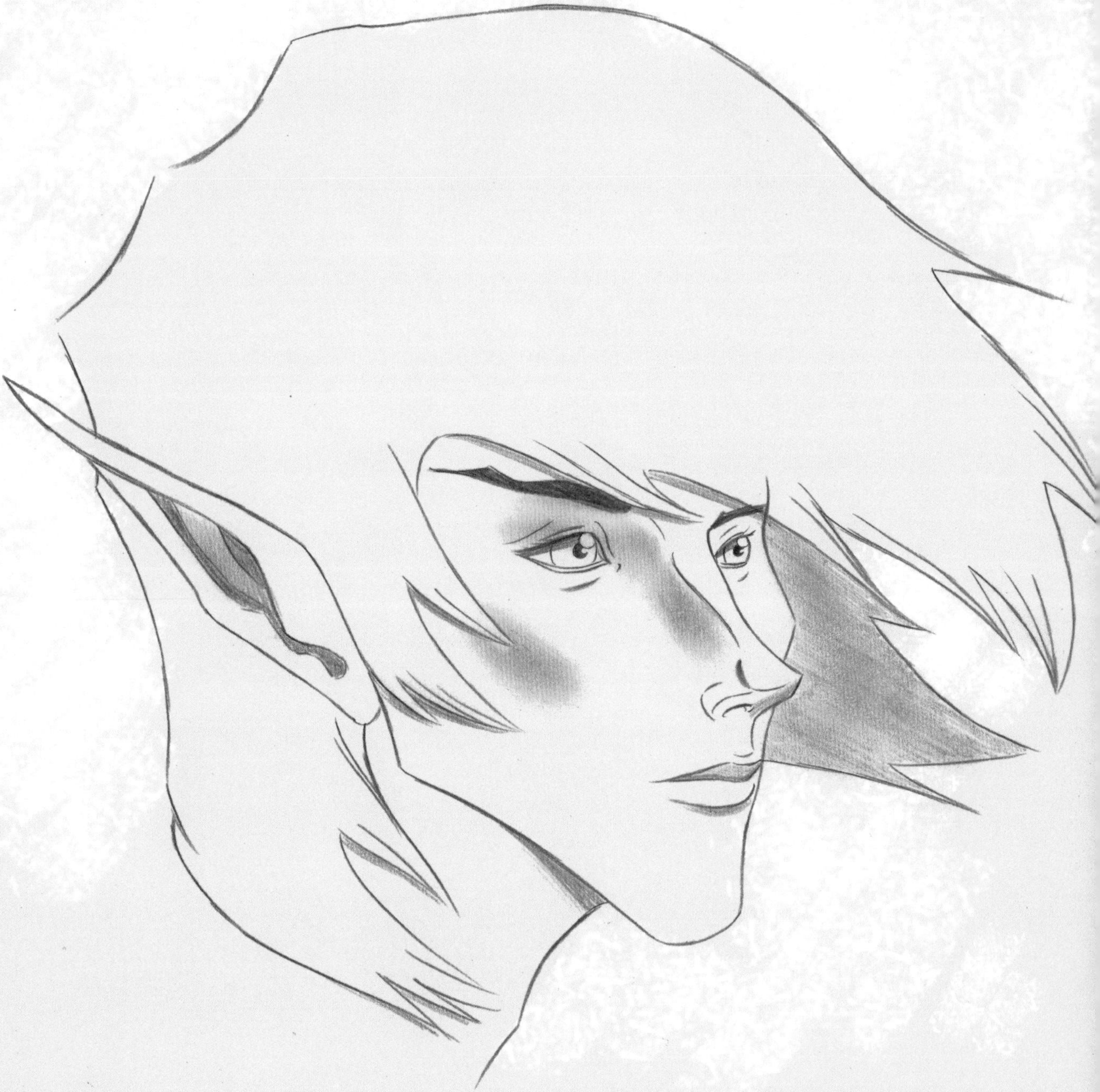

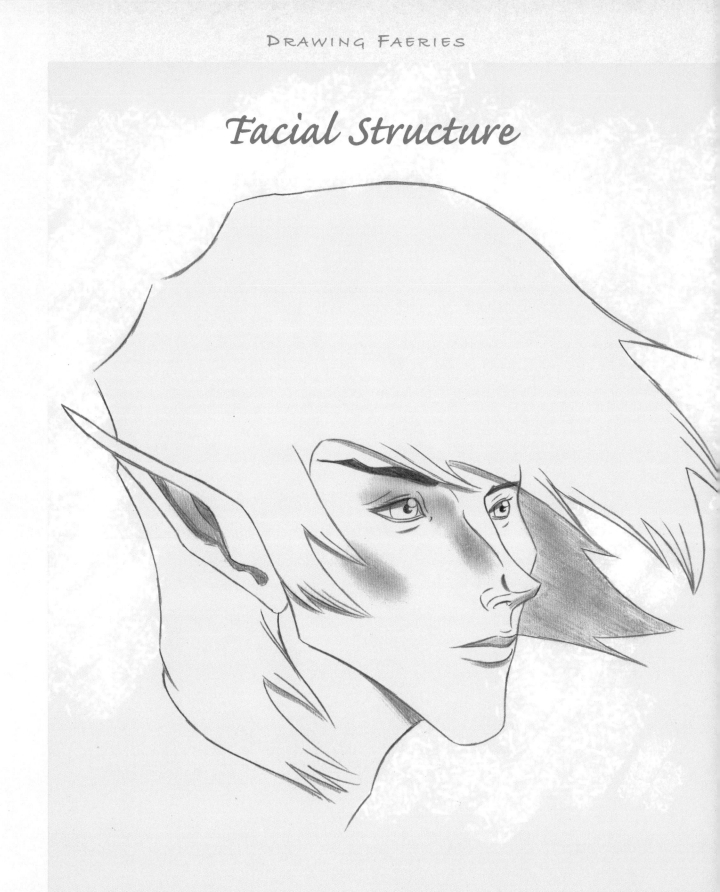

The faerie head is quite slender. Male faeries in particular have a somewhat angular face, with a pronounced chin and cheekbones. The facial structure is drawn without any hint of aggression or brutishness.

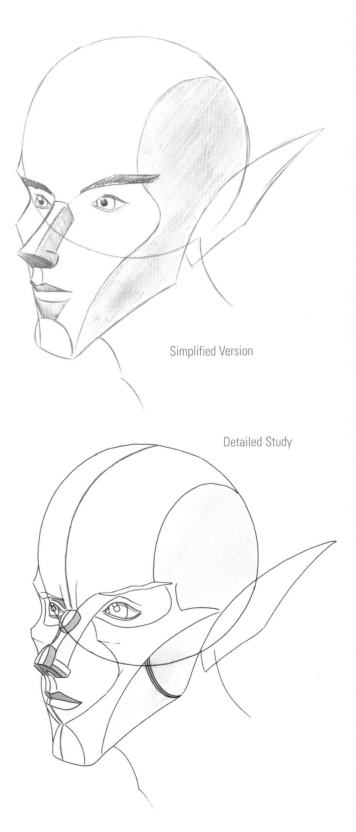

Simplified Version

Detailed Study

The general structure of the skull shows the high cheekbone (zygomatic arch), the jaw muscle (mastoid process), and protruding forms, such as the nose, lips, and chin.

The Head in Profile

The profile is known among artists as a generally unflattering pose, because it provides a rather harsh, flat, and unforgiving view of the subject. But you can cast those considerations aside when it comes to faerie folk. In fact, the profile is a particularly attractive angle at which to draw faeries, as it emphasizes their sleek lines. It reveals the faerie's high jaw, delicate chin, and upturned nose. Note how the ear is drawn at a sharp, forty-five degree diagonal.

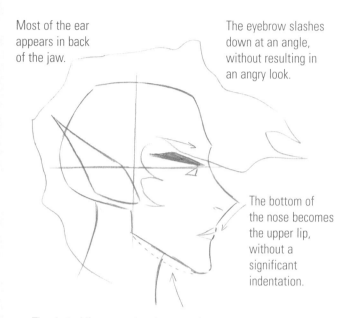

Most of the ear appears in back of the jaw.

The eyebrow slashes down at an angle, without resulting in an angry look.

The bottom of the nose becomes the upper lip, without a significant indentation.

The dotted line connotes the normal jawline for humans, which is fuller than it is for faeries.

Basic Anatomy

The faeries' underlying anatomy is remarkable. It seems that, for adaptive reasons, they have evolved a more angular skull. One assumes that it bestows some advantage upon them. I have conjectured that their subtle skull configuration requires less mass than the heavier configuration of the human skull. Their lightness translates into greater speed—a necessity for beings that rely upon stealth for their existence.

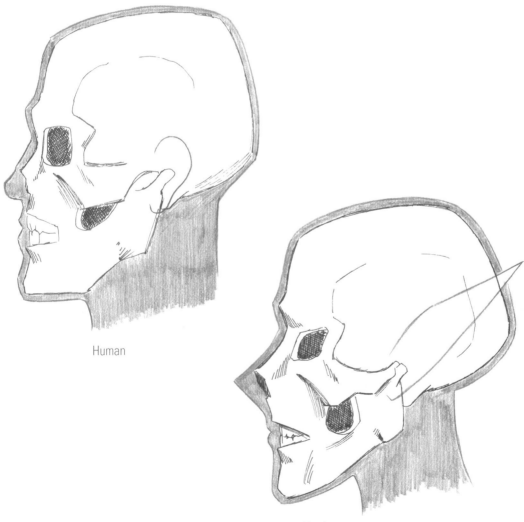

Human

Faerie

Female Faeries

I chose this nubile faerie as a sketch subject because of her simple beauty. Her eyes reflect a degree of self-composure that I found surprising for one so young. I quietly observed her near the lower gardens, and put pencil to paper for a quick sketch of her head. Many gentleman faeries came to call on her during that afternoon. She rebuffed all of their advances but seemed to enjoy the attention.

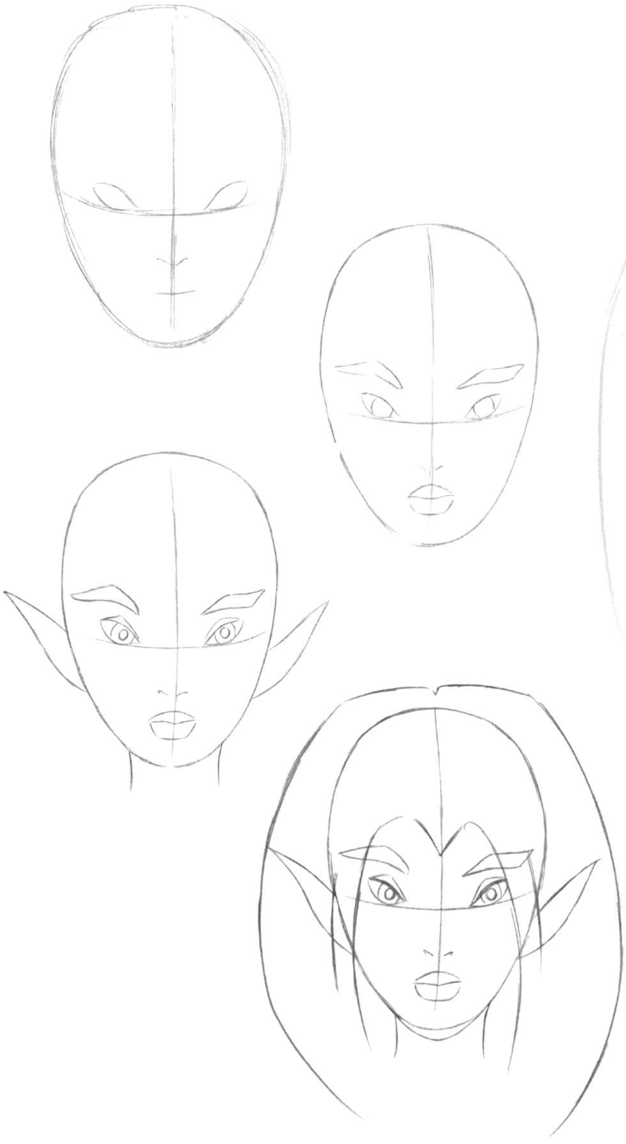

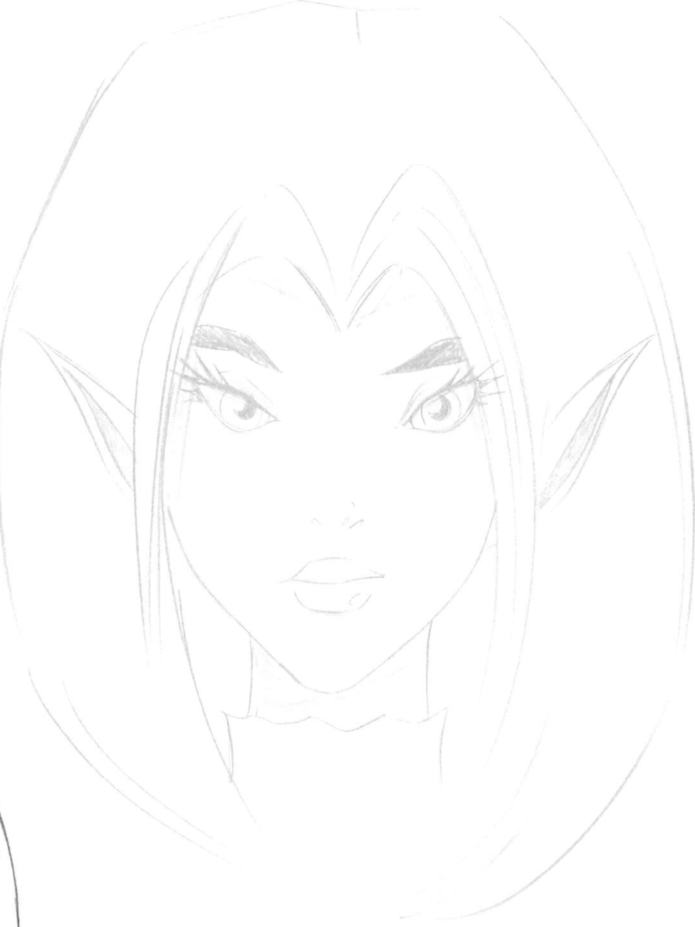

The female faerie's head begins as an egg shape, but tapers to, and is somewhat lengthened at, the chin.

Faerie Princess

You can feel the rapture of nature when looking into the eyes of a faerie princess. She is the warm summer breeze, the sweet smell of pine, the mist that rises with the morning dew. Next time you walk through a field of blossoms (something I highly recommend), and a row of flowers bows in succession, blown by a gentle wind, look quickly, for you just might see her frolicking among the blooms.

Her eyes are typically faerie in shape, long and raised at the ends.

The nose has a small, quick turn up at the tip.

Her lips are full and pensive.

An Uncommon Faerie

Some faeries have mouths that are set quite low on the face, which gives them an interesting look. It serves to diminish the size of the chin, and a small chin is considered to be a very desirable feature.

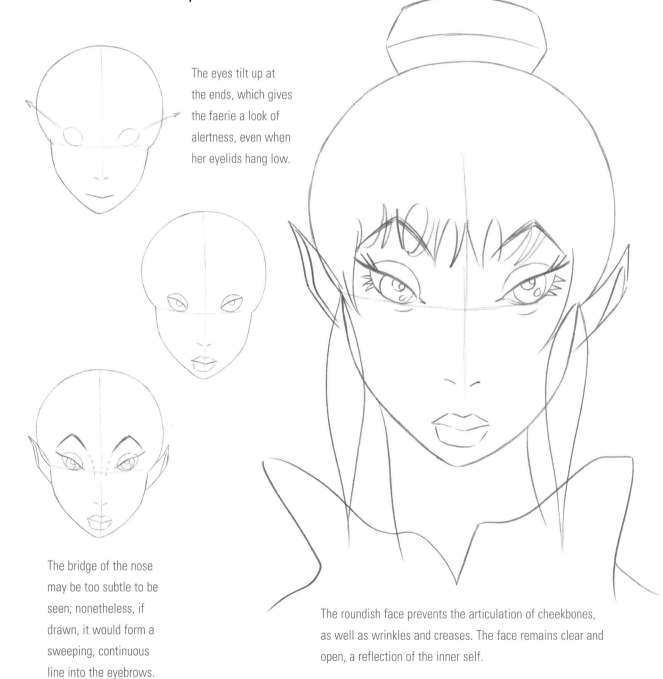

The eyes tilt up at the ends, which gives the faerie a look of alertness, even when her eyelids hang low.

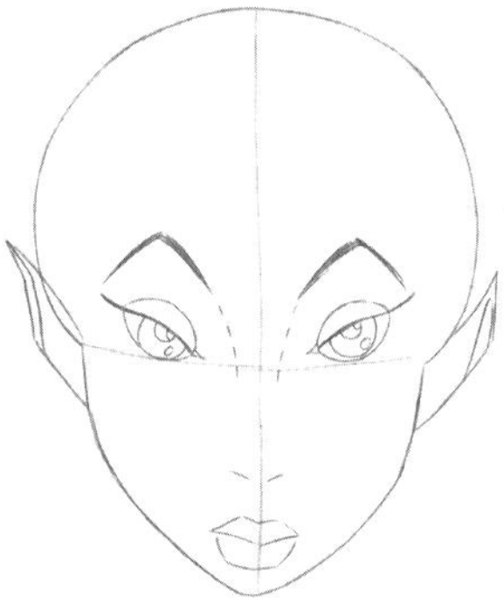

The bridge of the nose may be too subtle to be seen; nonetheless, if drawn, it would form a sweeping, continuous line into the eyebrows.

The roundish face prevents the articulation of cheekbones, as well as wrinkles and creases. The face remains clear and open, a reflection of the inner self.

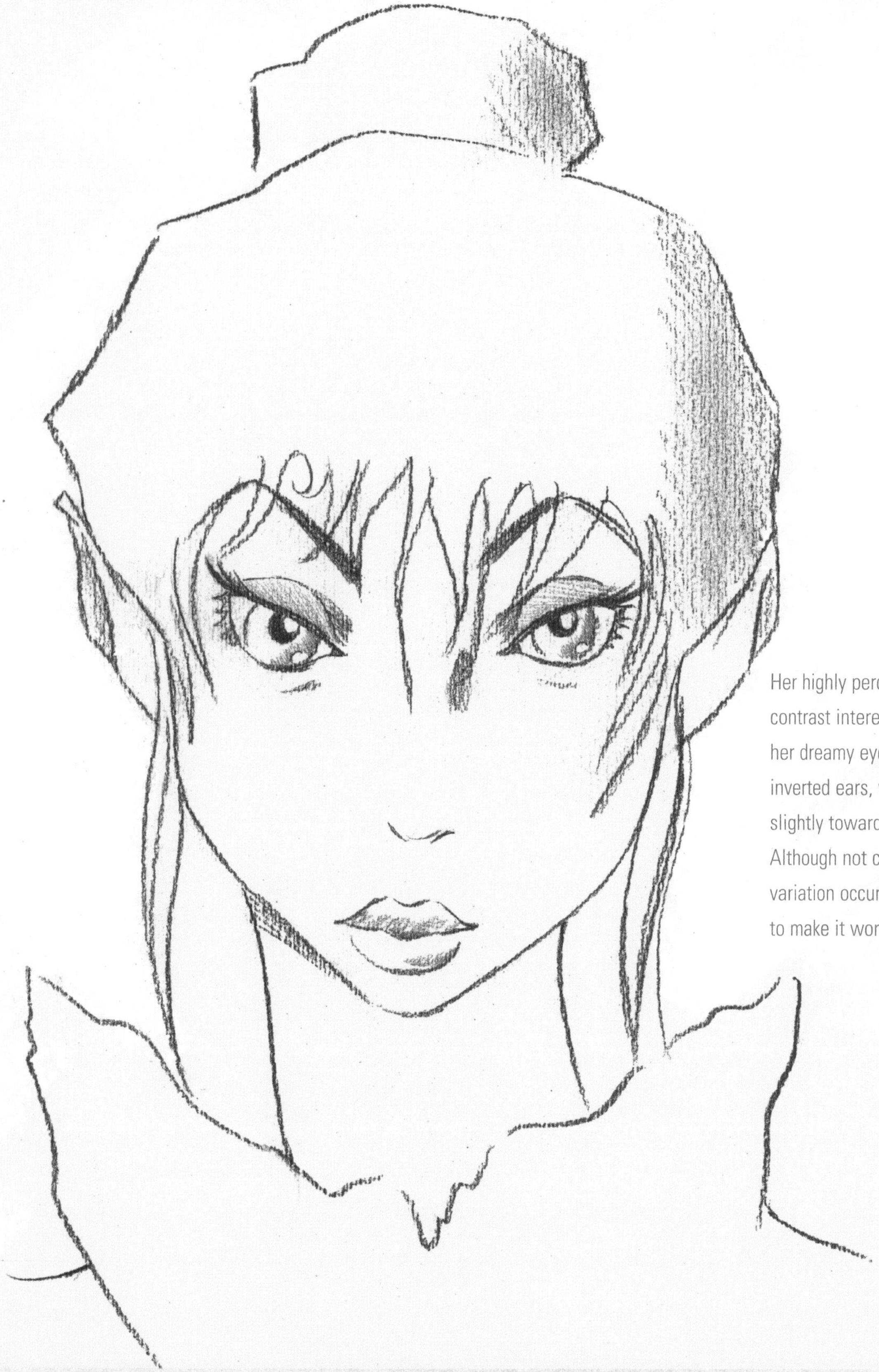

Her highly perched eyebrows contrast interestingly with her dreamy eyes. Note her inverted ears, which are turned slightly toward the rear. Although not common, this variation occurs often enough to make it worth noting.

Head Tilts

A simple turn of the head may result in a striking pose. The subtle angularity of faerie faces creates endless dramatic possibilities. Here is a good example of an upward head tilt, which foreshortens the nose and accentuates the size of the chin. In this position, the eyebrows become the top of the head, as the crown is obscured from view. It is essential to place the ears very low when the head is in this position.

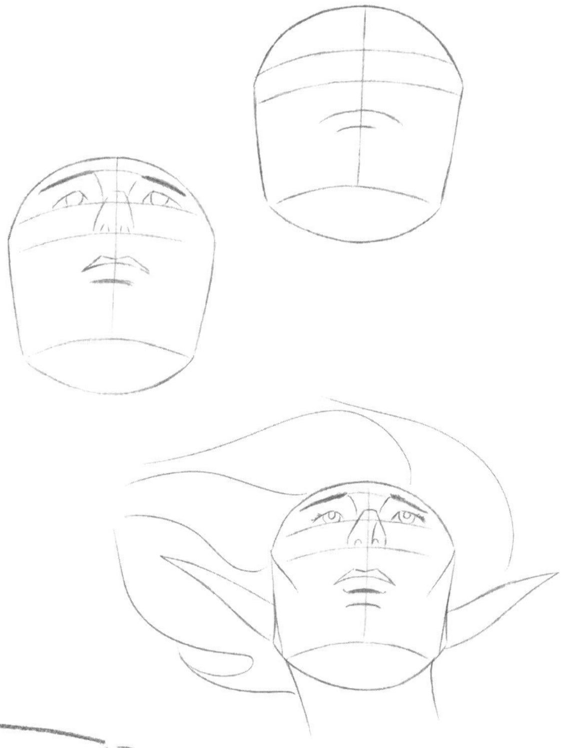

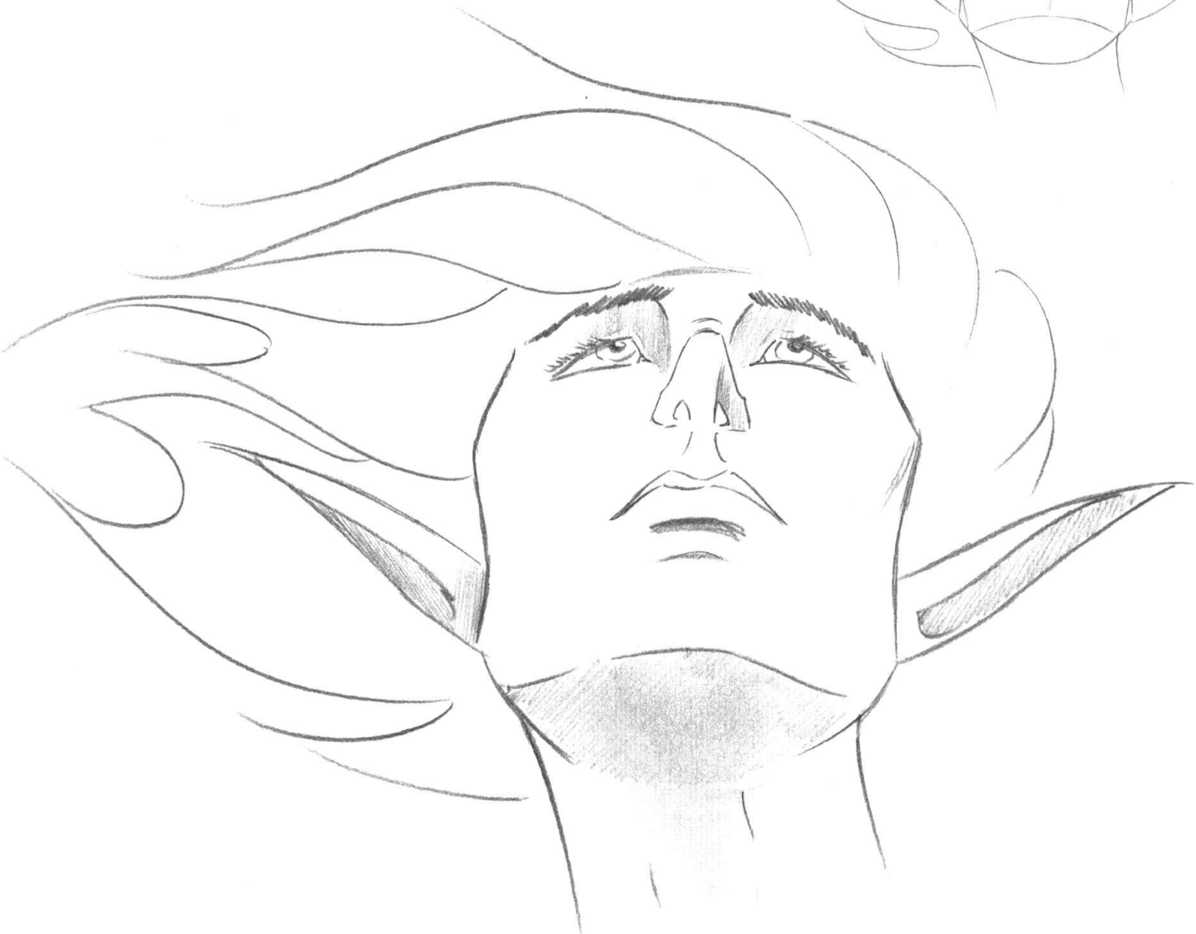

Here are a few more examples of head tilts, each with varying degrees of foreshortening.

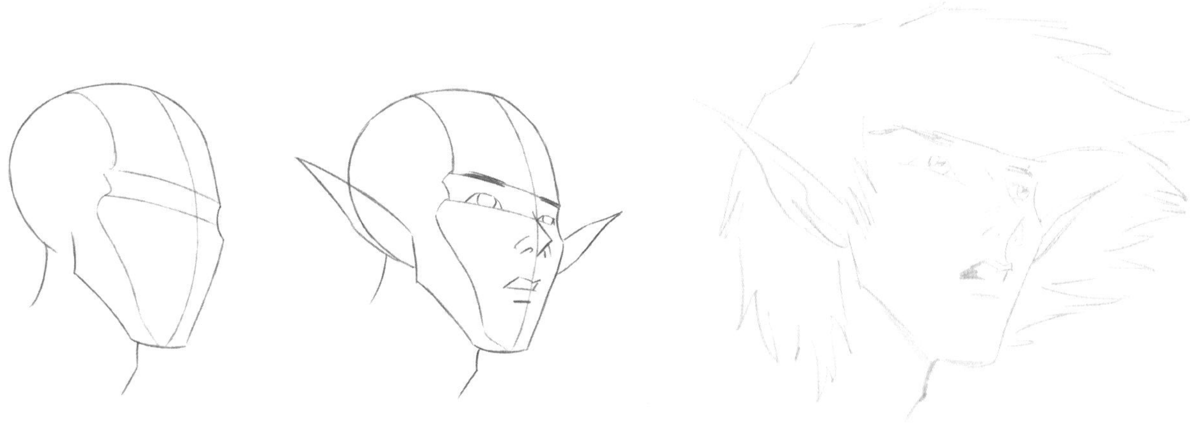

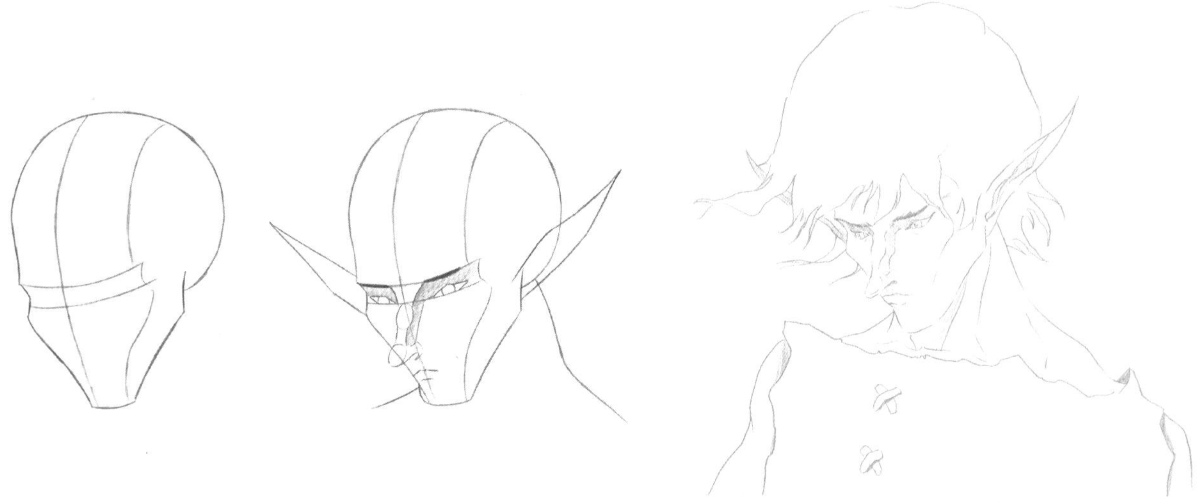

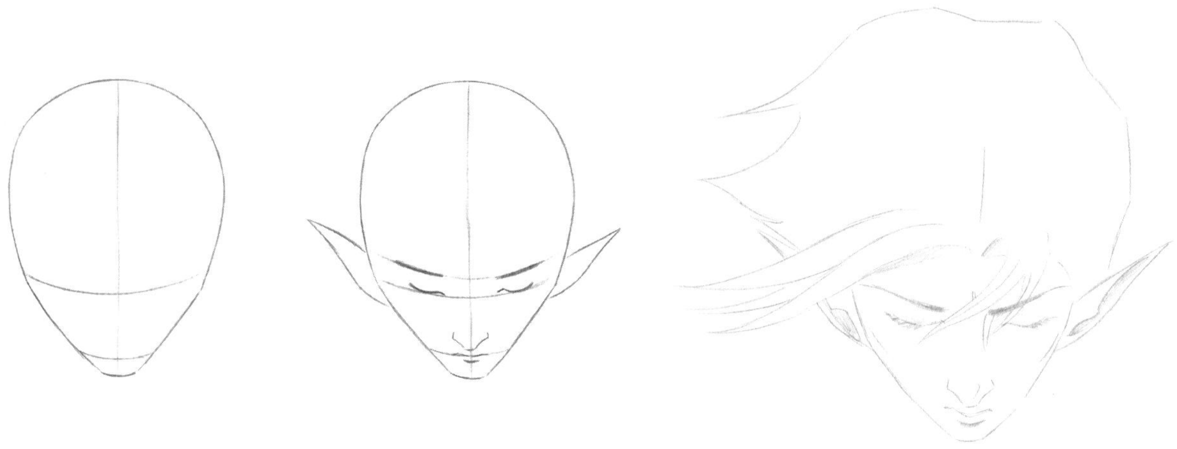

Showing Emotions

Faeries are very emotional creatures, though they shy away from overt displays. They believe that clinging to a feeling is an act of selfishness that might prevent the feeling from going to the next person, who might enjoy it. Instead, faeries allow feelings to wash over them; they experience the emotion and then pass it on to others.

Nonetheless, faeries do have many expressions, which I have attempted to capture on paper. Fortunately for you and me, their faces cannot hide emotions, as they are incapable of guile, except as is necessary in securing themselves from discovery. When not experiencing a specific emotion, their look is one of detached contentment.

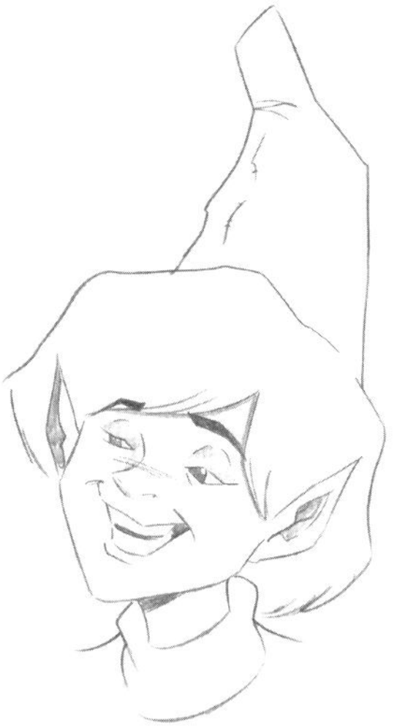
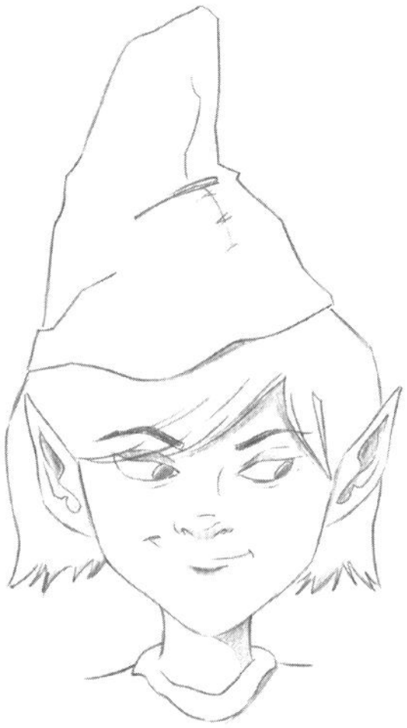
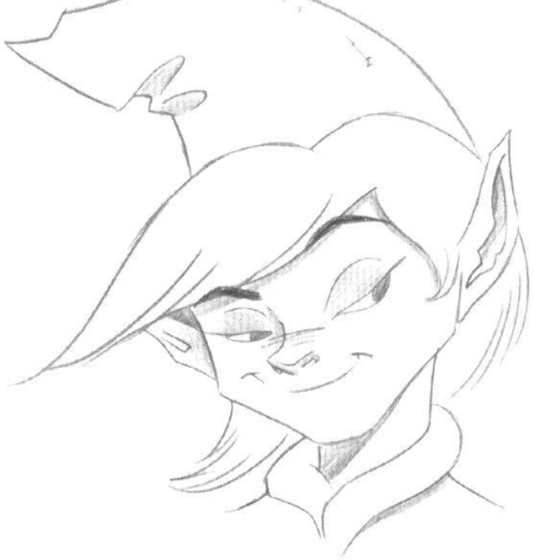
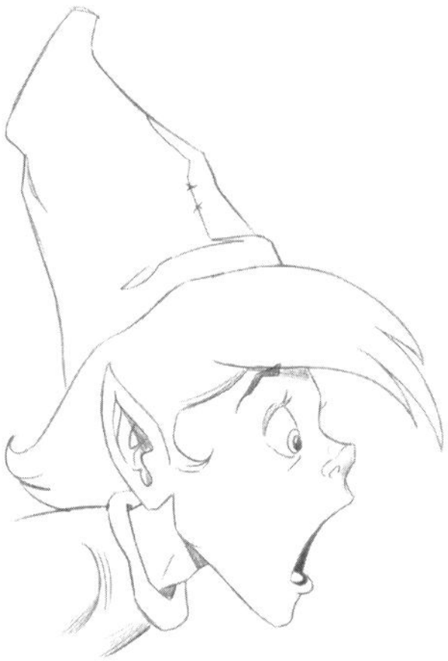
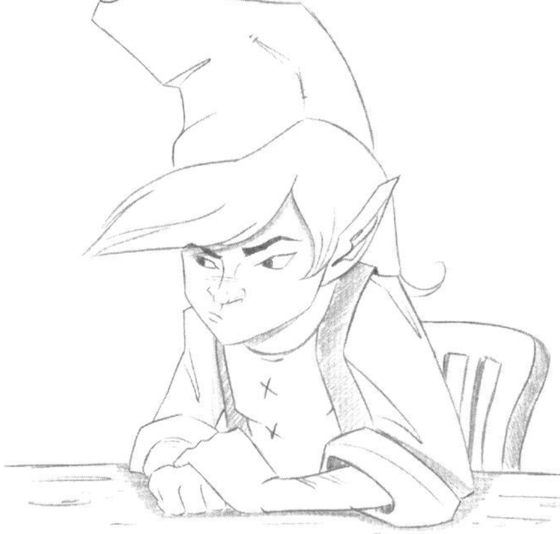
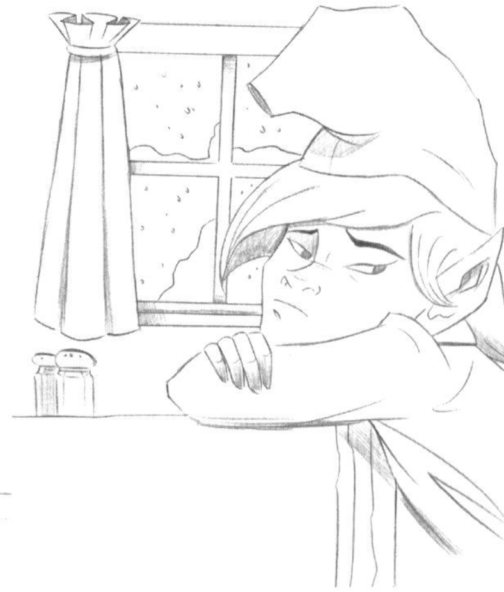

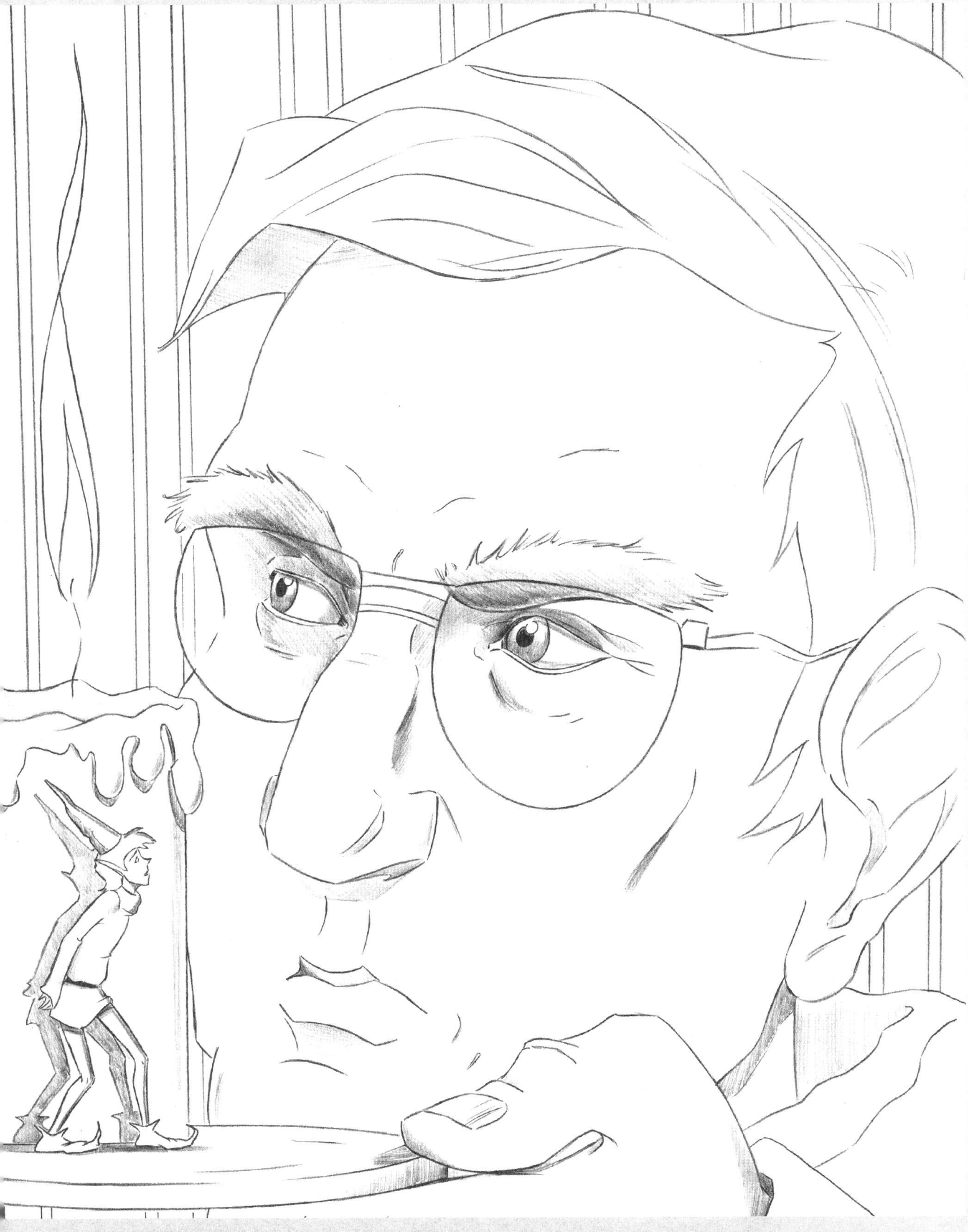

Drawing the Body

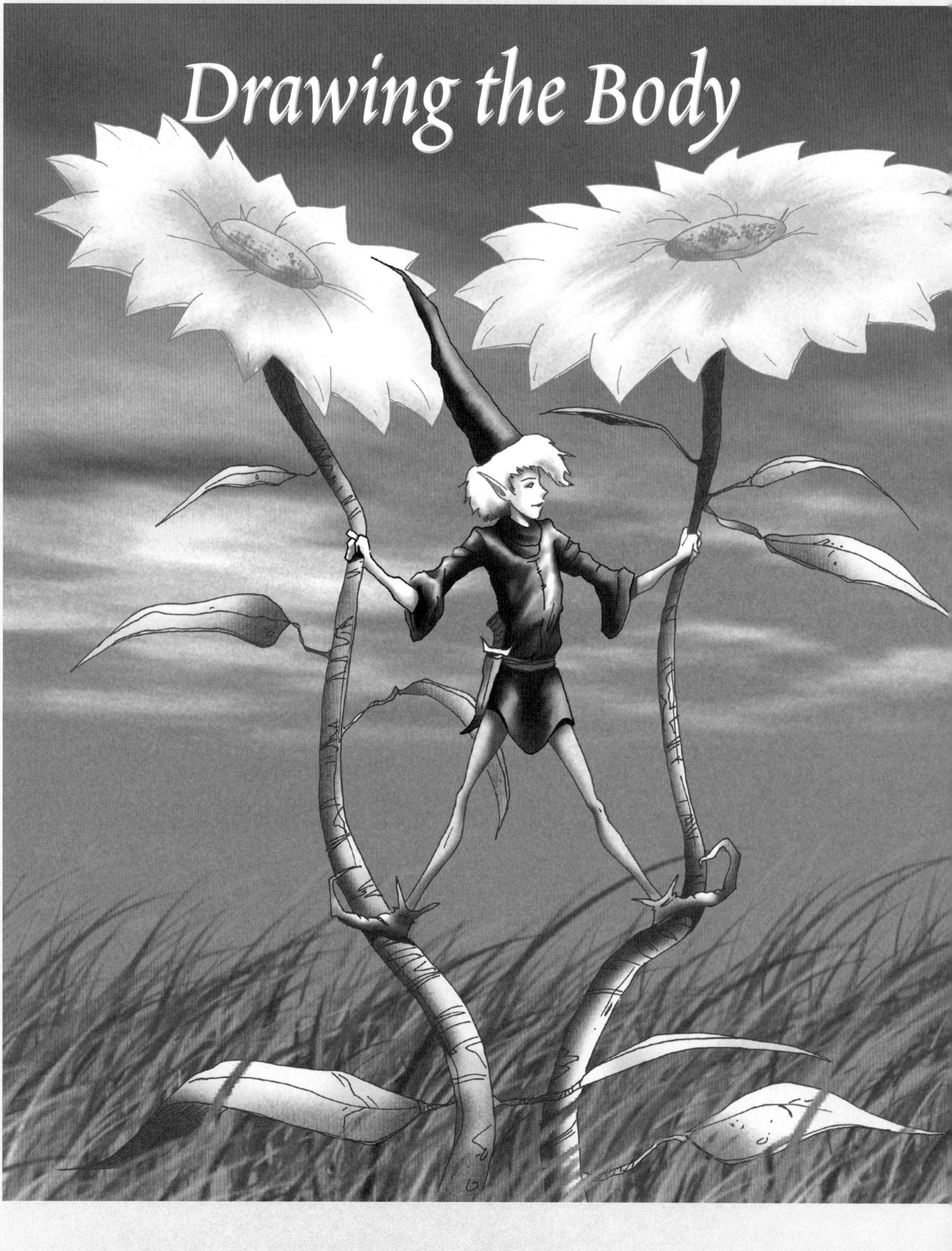

Proportions

Long and lithe, thin, even skinny—these are some of the adjectives that come to mind when drawing the faerie body. However, looks can be deceiving: Faeries are actually stronger than humans when their relative size is taken into account. In addition, faeries are proportionally considerably longer limbed than humans. You'll notice the difference between the arm lengths in the drawing at left.

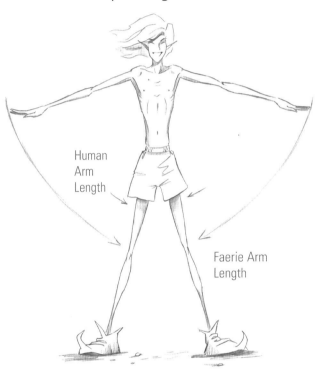

Human Arm Length

Faerie Arm Length

The Front Although the faerie body is quite thin, it is, at the same time, well shaped with long, sinewy muscles—not weight-lifter muscles, but the muscles of a swimmer.

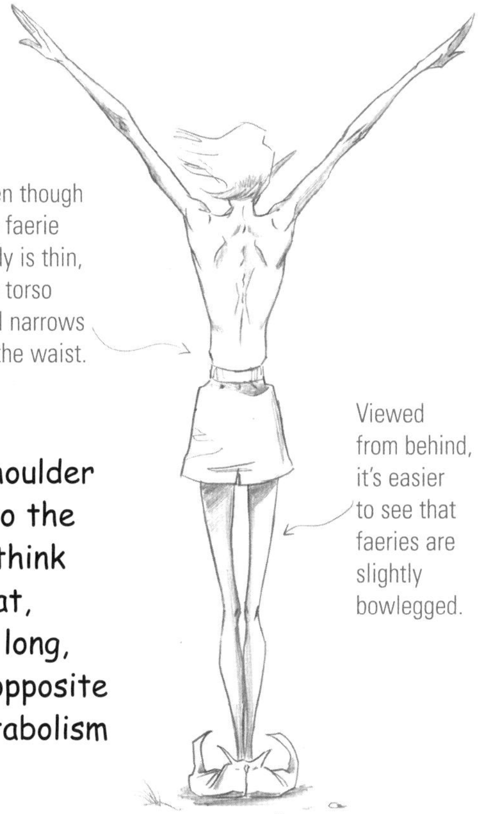

Even though the faerie body is thin, the torso still narrows at the waist.

Viewed from behind, it's easier to see that faeries are slightly bowlegged.

The Back The spine and the shoulder blades are quite pronounced, due to the lack of any excess fat. You might think that faeries, with such low body fat, would positively freeze during the long, cold winter months. Actually, the opposite is the case, as their increased metabolism keeps them comfortably warm.

Female Bodies

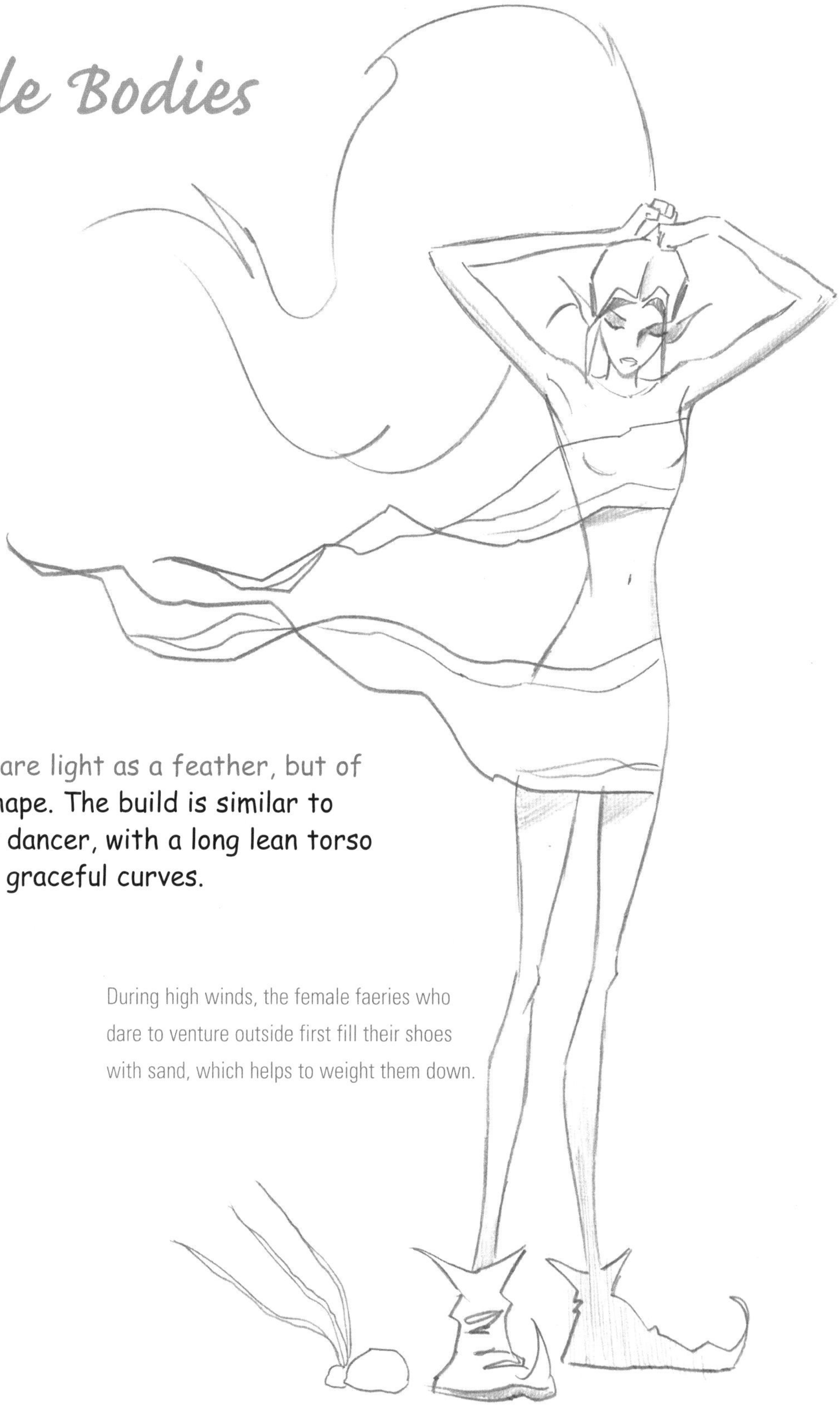

Female faeries are light as a feather, but of an attractive shape. The build is similar to that of a ballet dancer, with a long lean torso and modest yet graceful curves.

During high winds, the female faeries who dare to venture outside first fill their shoes with sand, which helps to weight them down.

We tend to think of human proportions as the "correct" ones. I hold no such prejudice. However, for the sake of comparison, I have no alternative but to use the human model. It is a well-accepted artistic axiom that the area just below the groin is the halfway point of the human body, when measured for height. But this is not so for faeries, as their legs take up a greater percentage of their overall length. This is another reason for their quickness and speed.

Gesture Sketches

Faeries are lively and quick, and have the ability to assume a variety of positions and poses that many humans would find challenging, and perhaps a little painful.

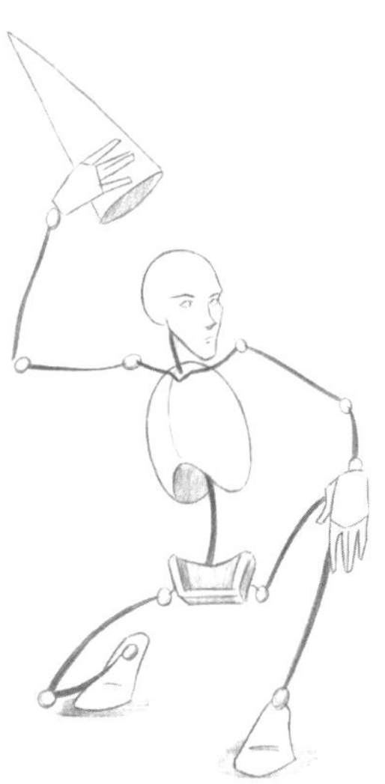

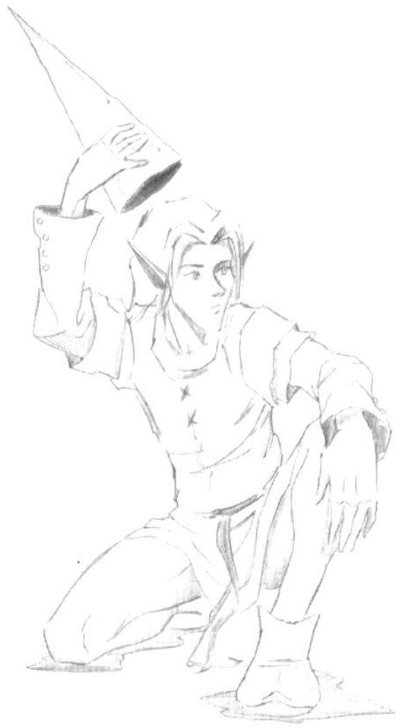

The Underlying Mechanics

Underlying every gesture, no matter how complex, there is a simple pose that can be stripped down to its essence. This artist's "shorthand" is comprised of a rib cage, a pelvis, and a simplified skeleton. It is not used so much in the actual practice of drawing, but as an aid to help the artist visualize the simplicity inherent in any gesture.

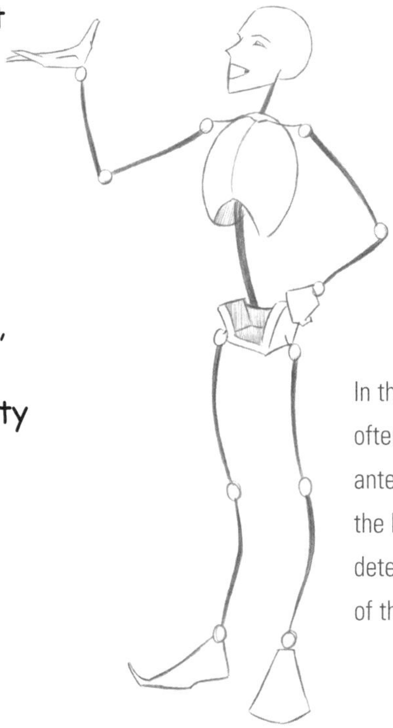

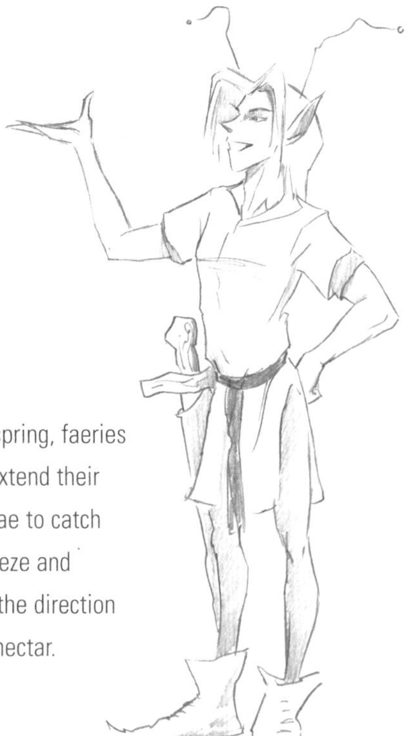

In the spring, faeries often extend their antennae to catch the breeze and detect the direction of the nectar.

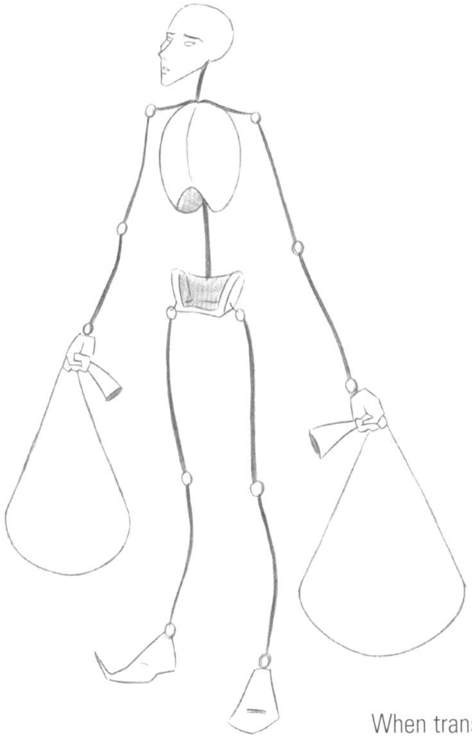

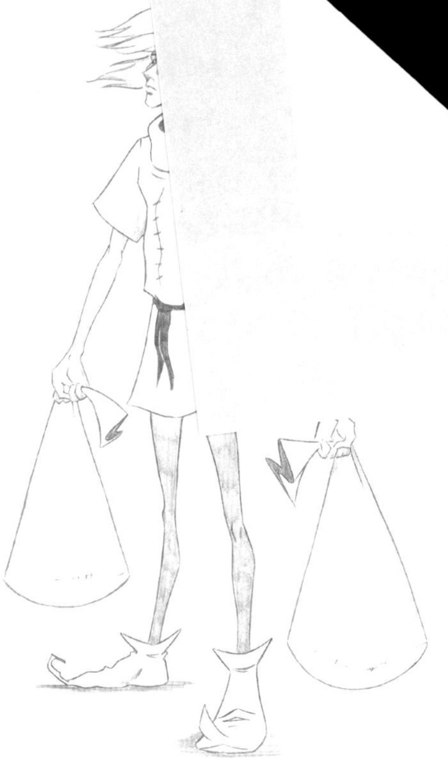

When translated into their primary and most essential elements, poses that seemed challenging become obvious and simple.

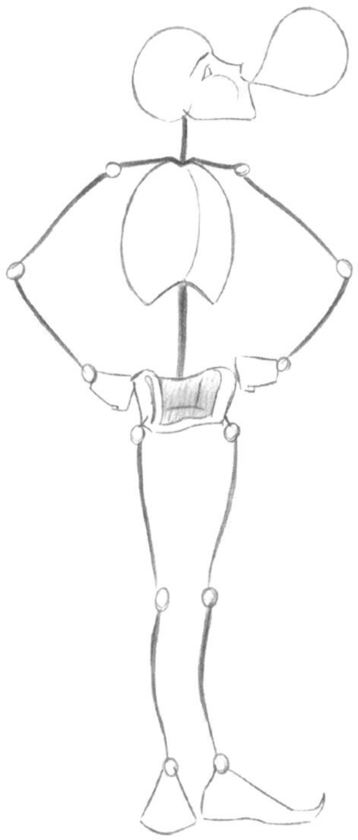

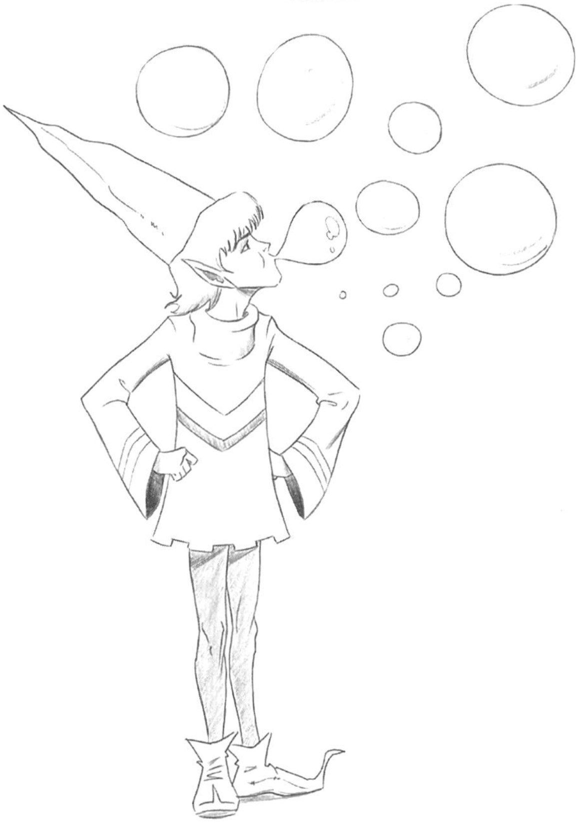

Blocking Out the Body

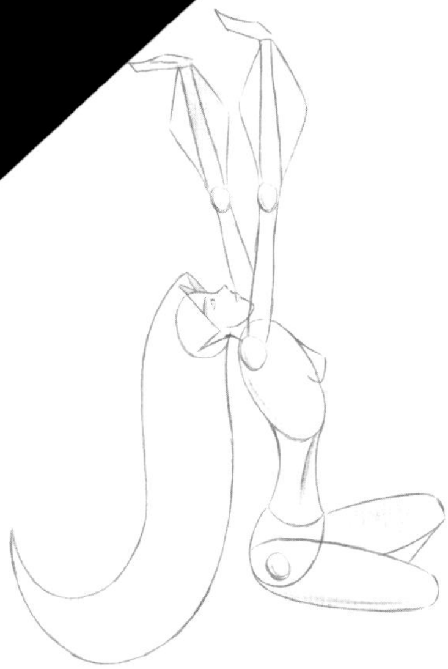

A more advanced yet, paradoxically, easier method than the former is to block out the body without resorting to using the simplified skeleton. The skeleton is still there, but the surface anatomy and contours are the focus. These constructions are commonly used as the basis for finished drawings.

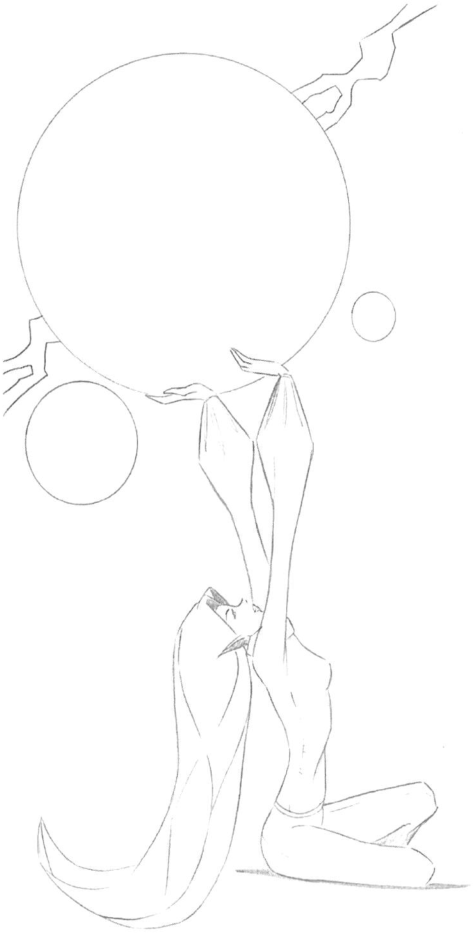

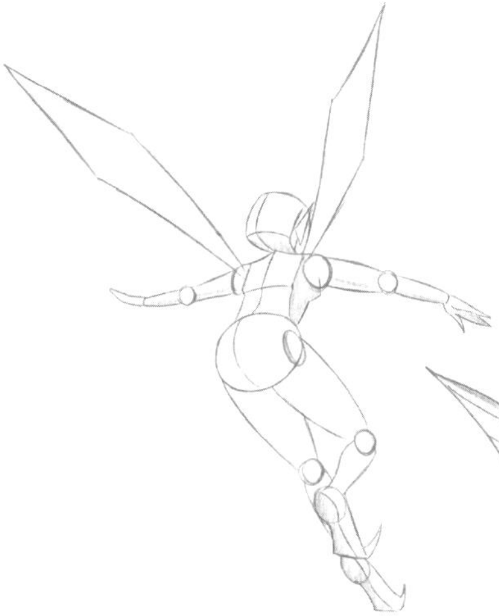

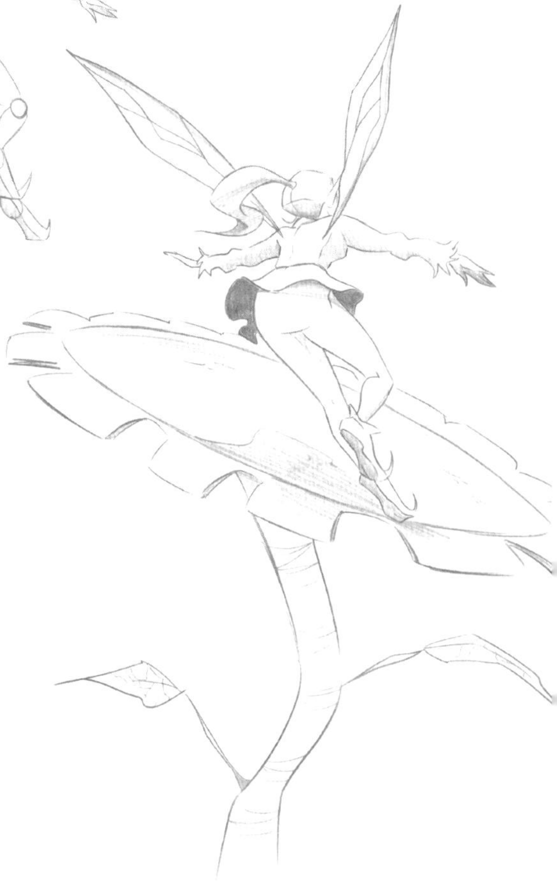

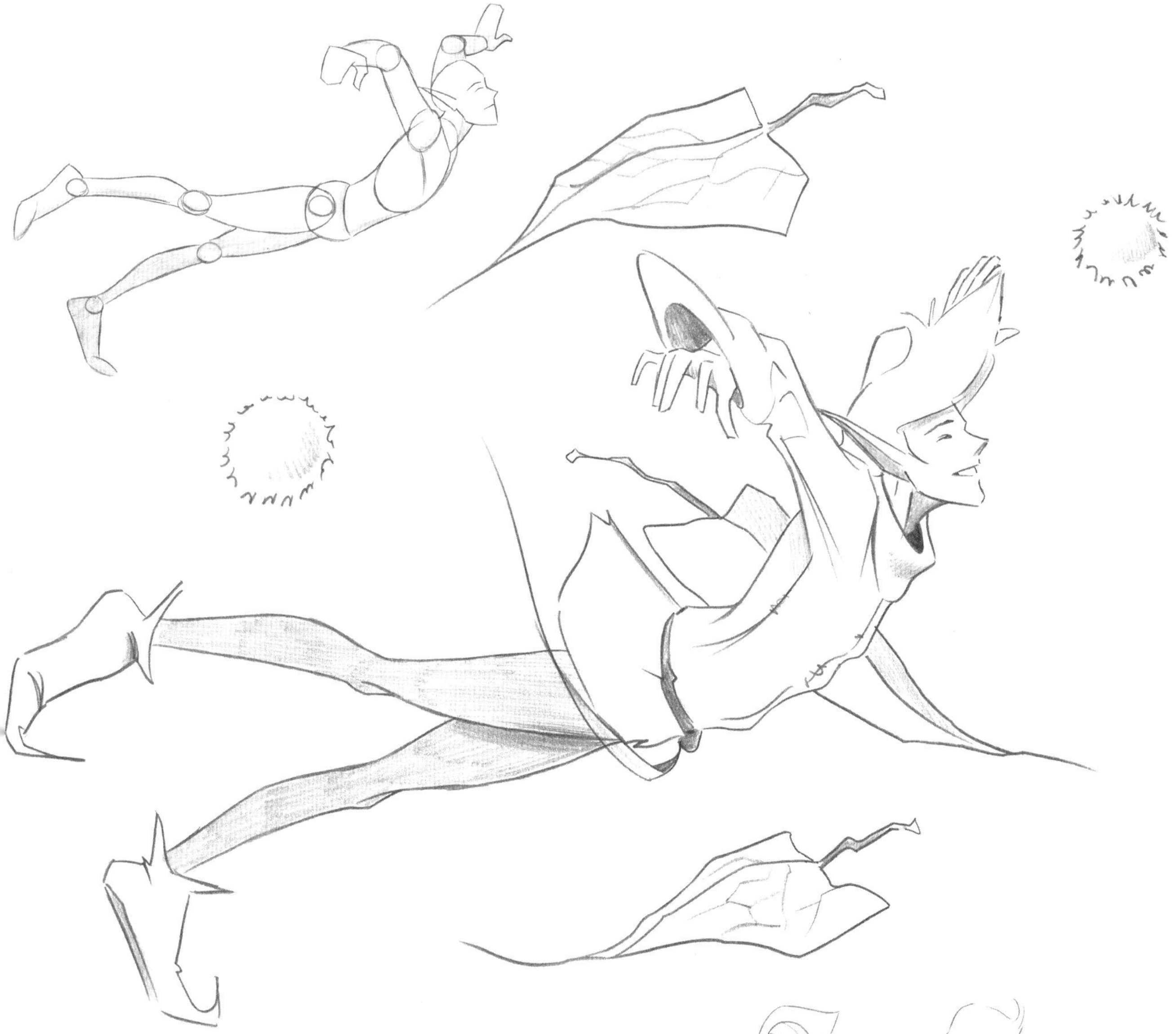

This would be, I suppose, the faerie equivalent of bungee jumping. In autumn, when I was a child, I would delight in jumping into a pile of leaves. But these fellows have turned it into an art. They become almost rapturous as they fall into the leaves from great heights.

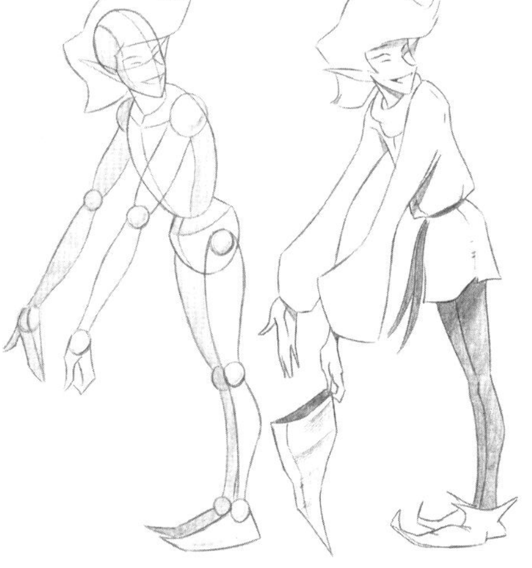

Morning Dew

It takes great patience to spy one of these nimble beings at the crack of dawn. They are as quick as humming-birds, and I had to return numerous times to complete my sketch. I wish I could simply set up a time-release exposure camera. But of course, faeries don't show up on film.

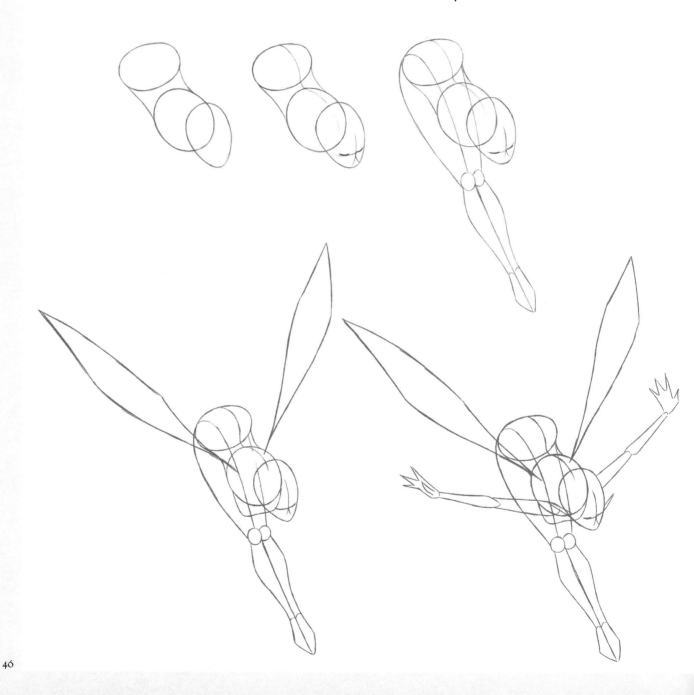

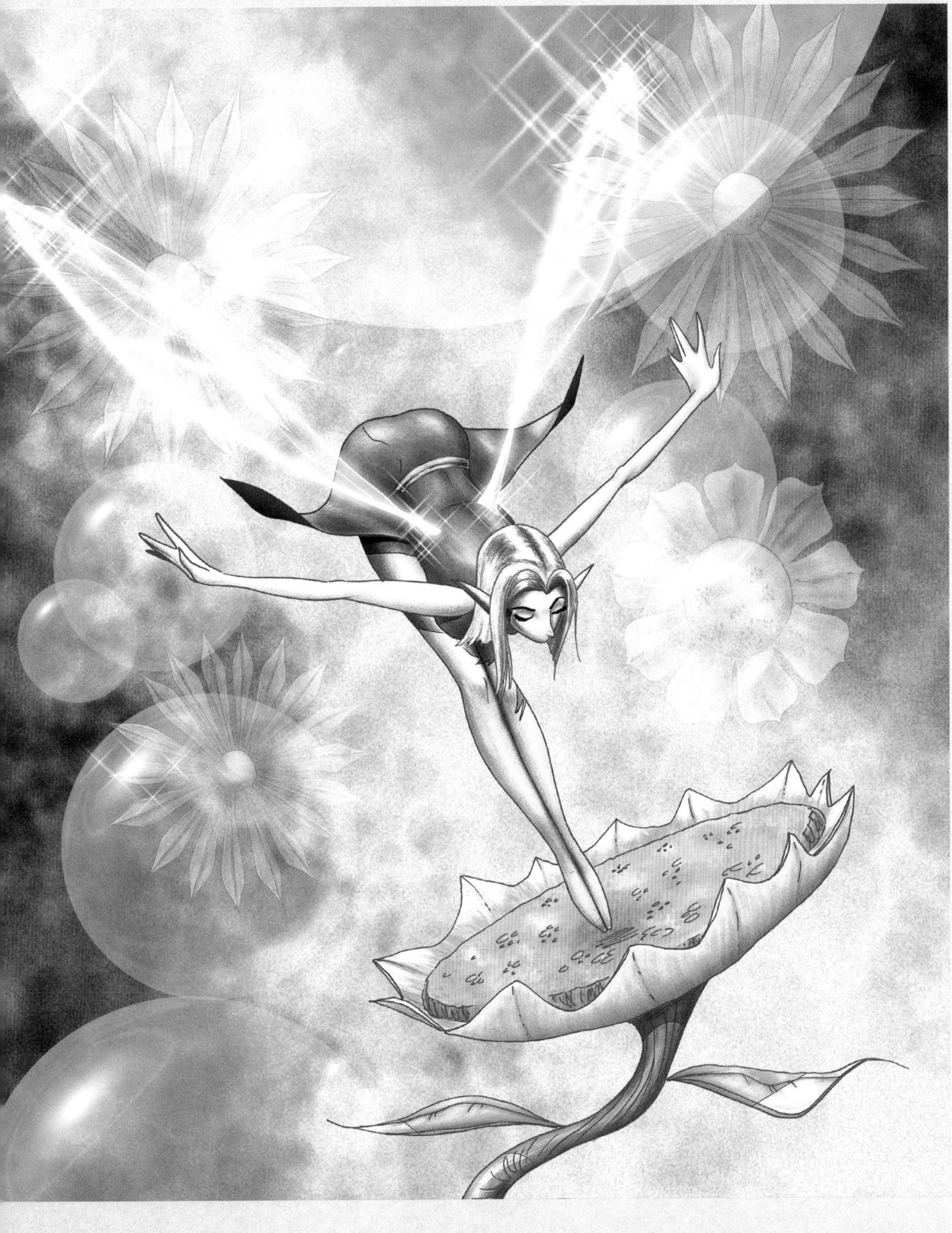

Rotations

To become familiar with a subject, it's essential to draw it from several angles. This is not an easy task with faeries, for they are elusive folk. I got lucky with this little fellow, who was debating whether to jump in for a swim or not.

A basic study can help set a pose. First reduce the figure to a simple model. Start with a light line drawing of the understructure, and then work the final figure, and clothing, on top of it.

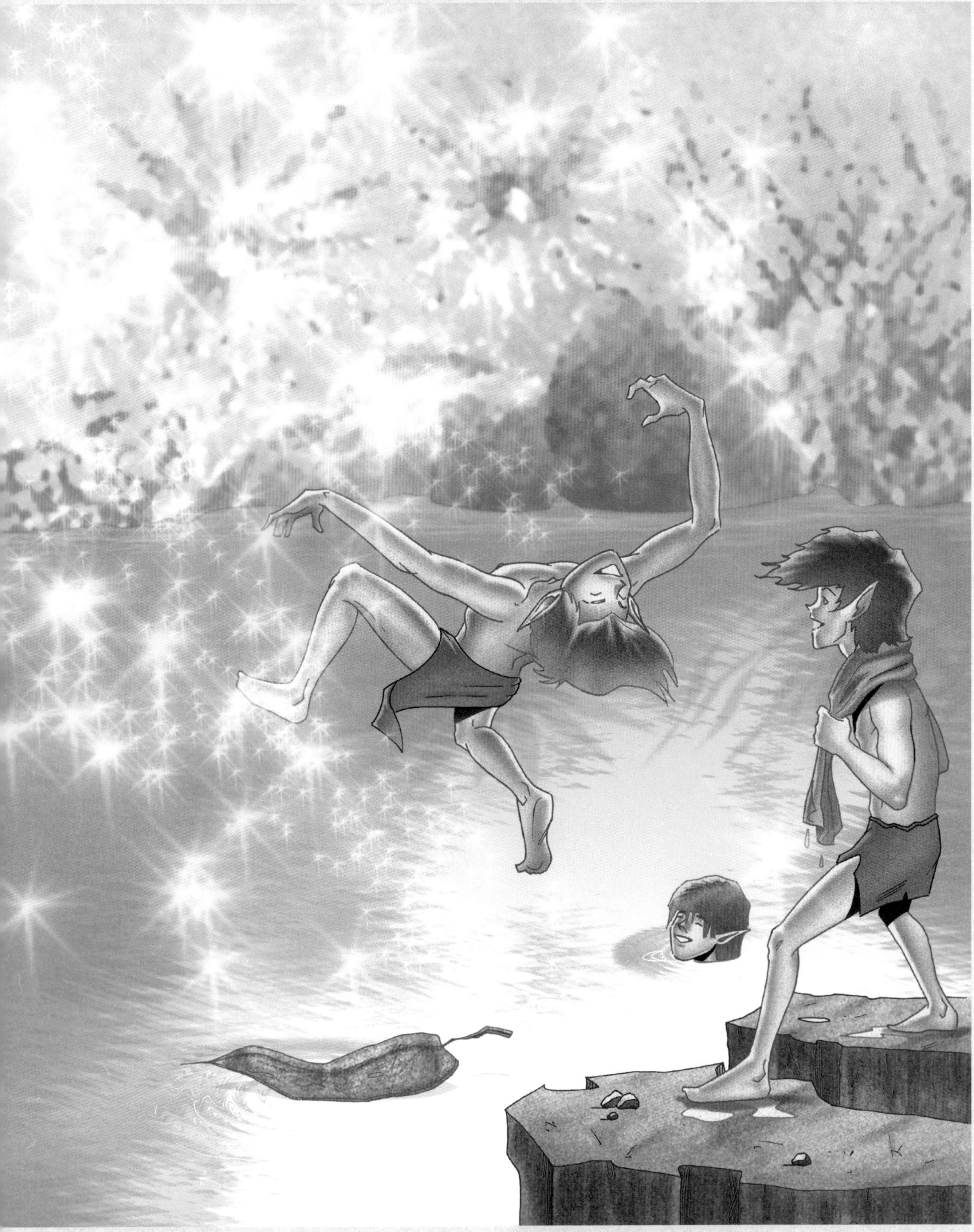

Flexibility

Faeries are quite loose limbed and tend to hyperextend as a matter of course. This gives them a greater range of motion.

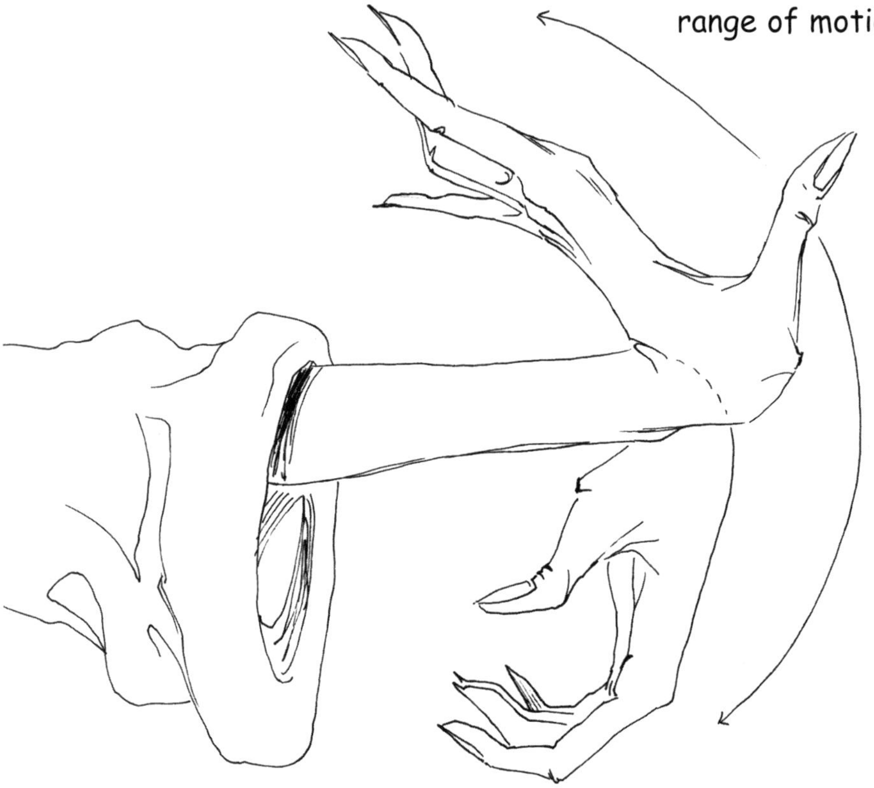

Increased flexibility provides for increased range of motion.

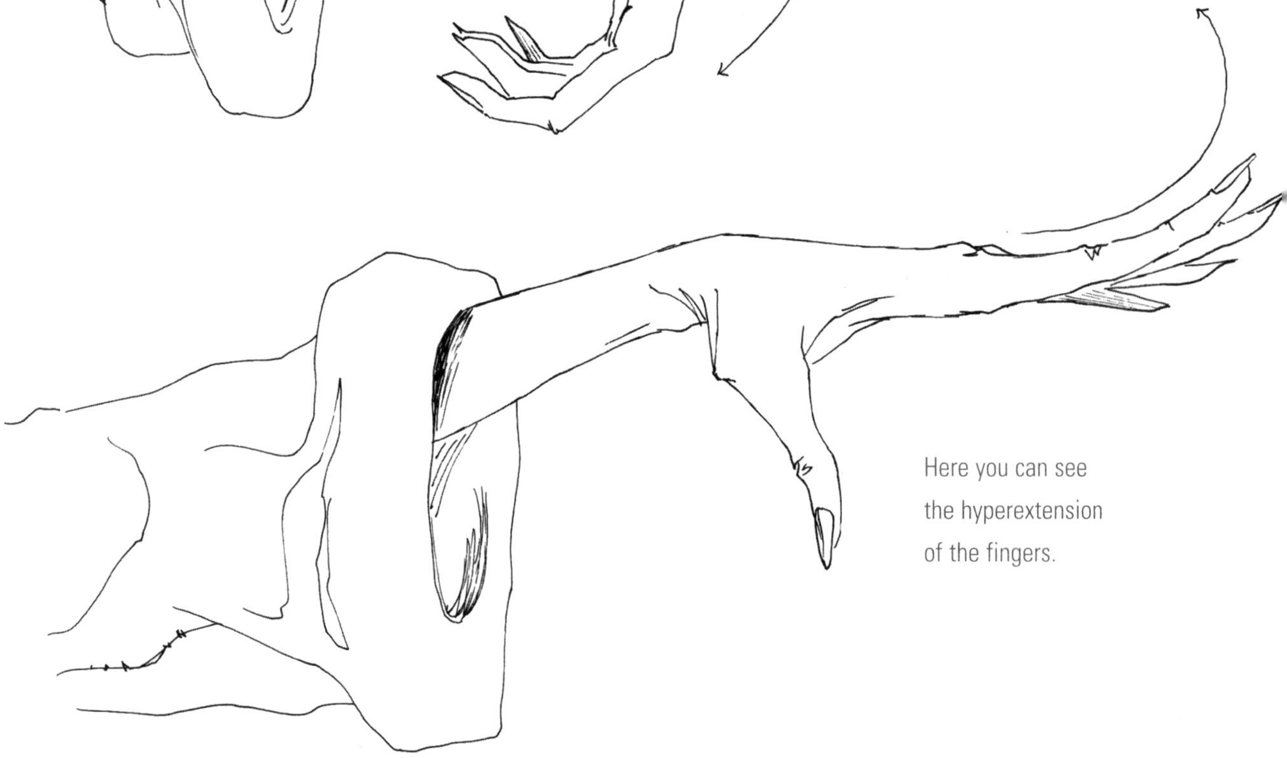

Here you can see the hyperextension of the fingers.

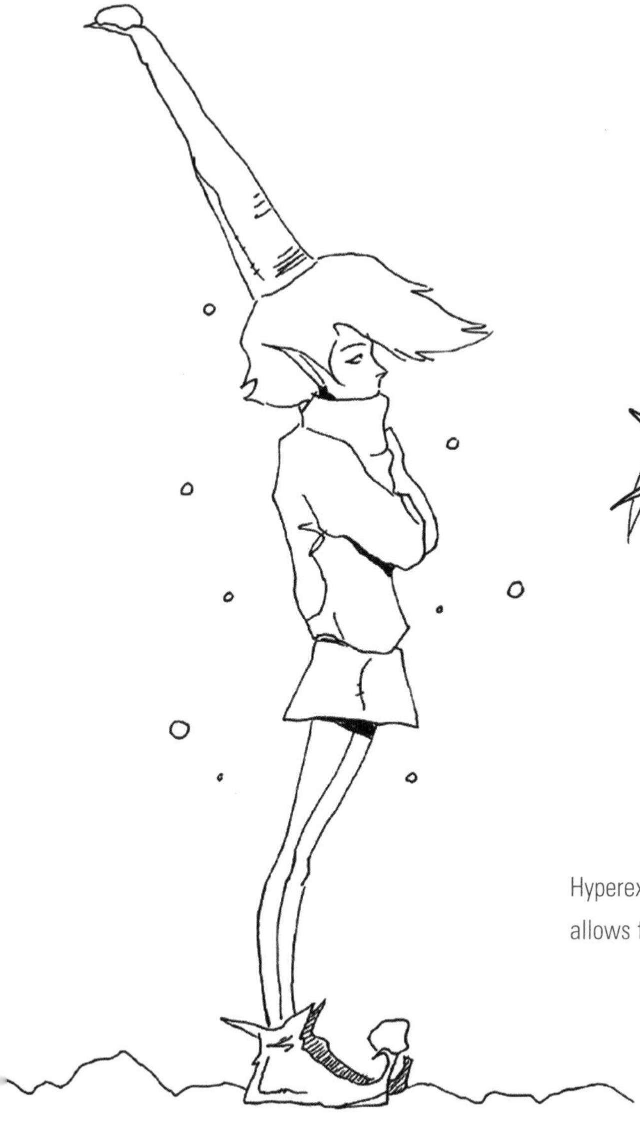

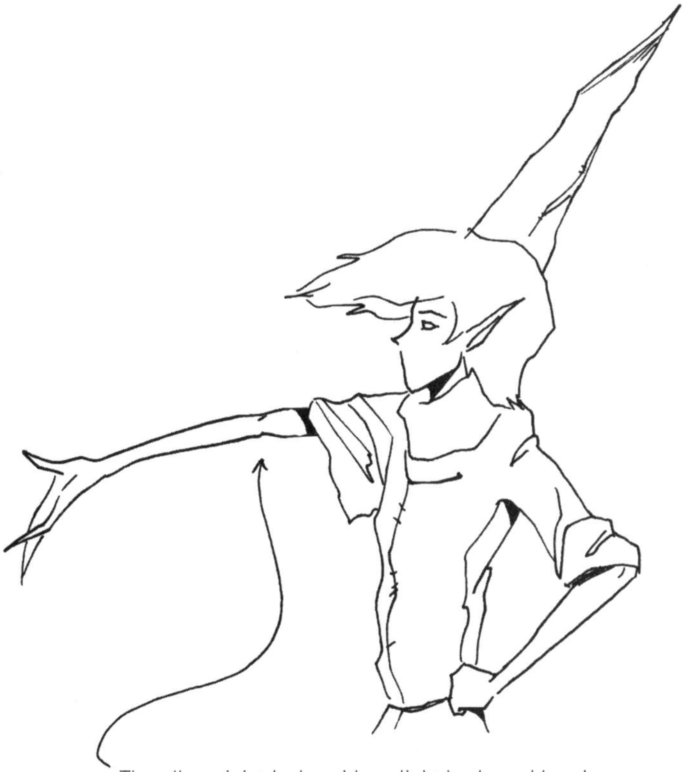

The elbow joint locks with a slight backward bend.

Hyperextension of the knees, when locked in the standing position, allows for the legs to bend slightly "in the wrong direction."

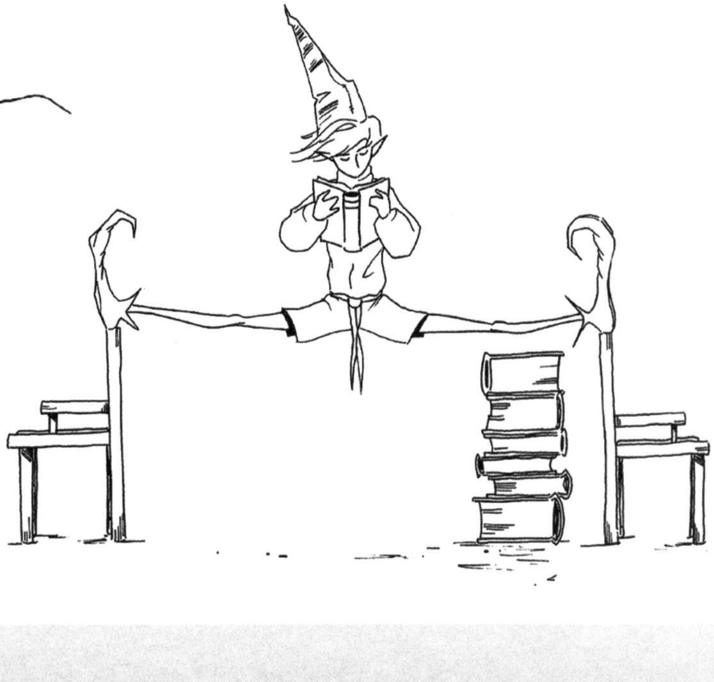

A natural flexibility allows faeries to assume positions that might be uncomfortable for all but the most adaptive humans.

Footnote

It is a well-known fact that faeries wear slip-on shoes that are pointed at the tips. What is generally not known, however, is that faeries wear this type of footwear because it is in the only shape that conforms to their feet. Faeries have extra-long big toes, which serve to enhance their balance. Unfortunately, it also makes for a rather narrow selection of shoe styles.

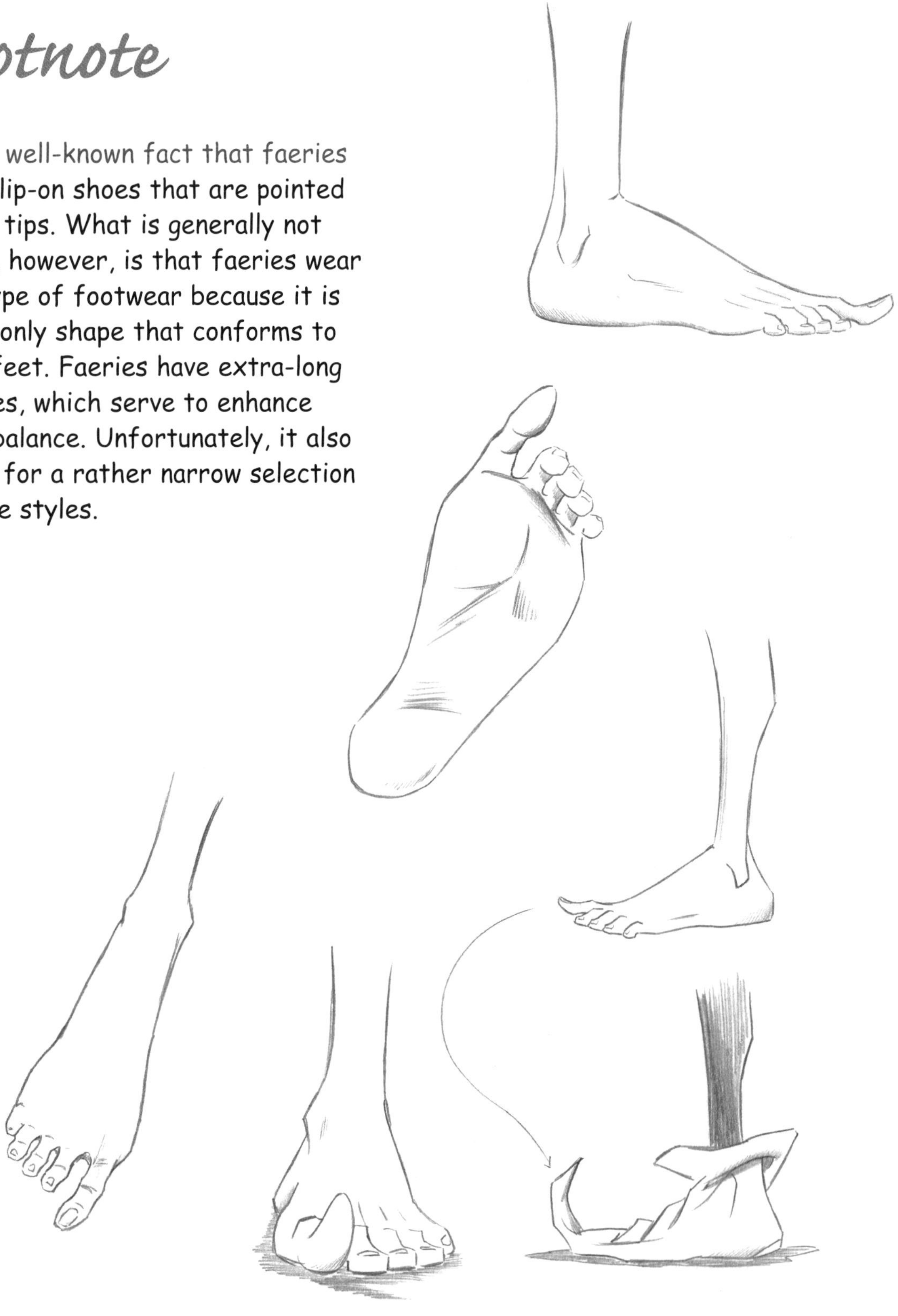

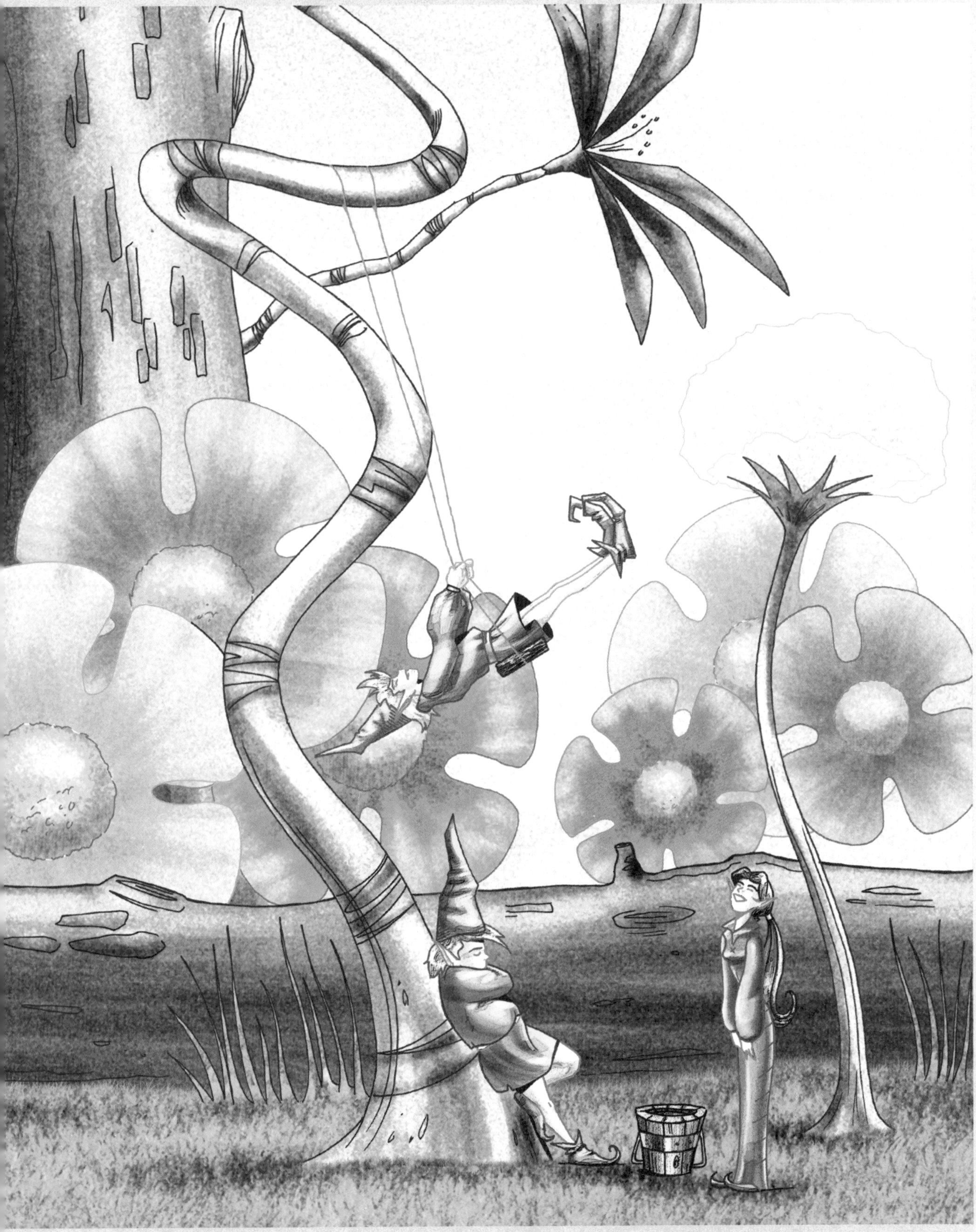

A Faerie's Life

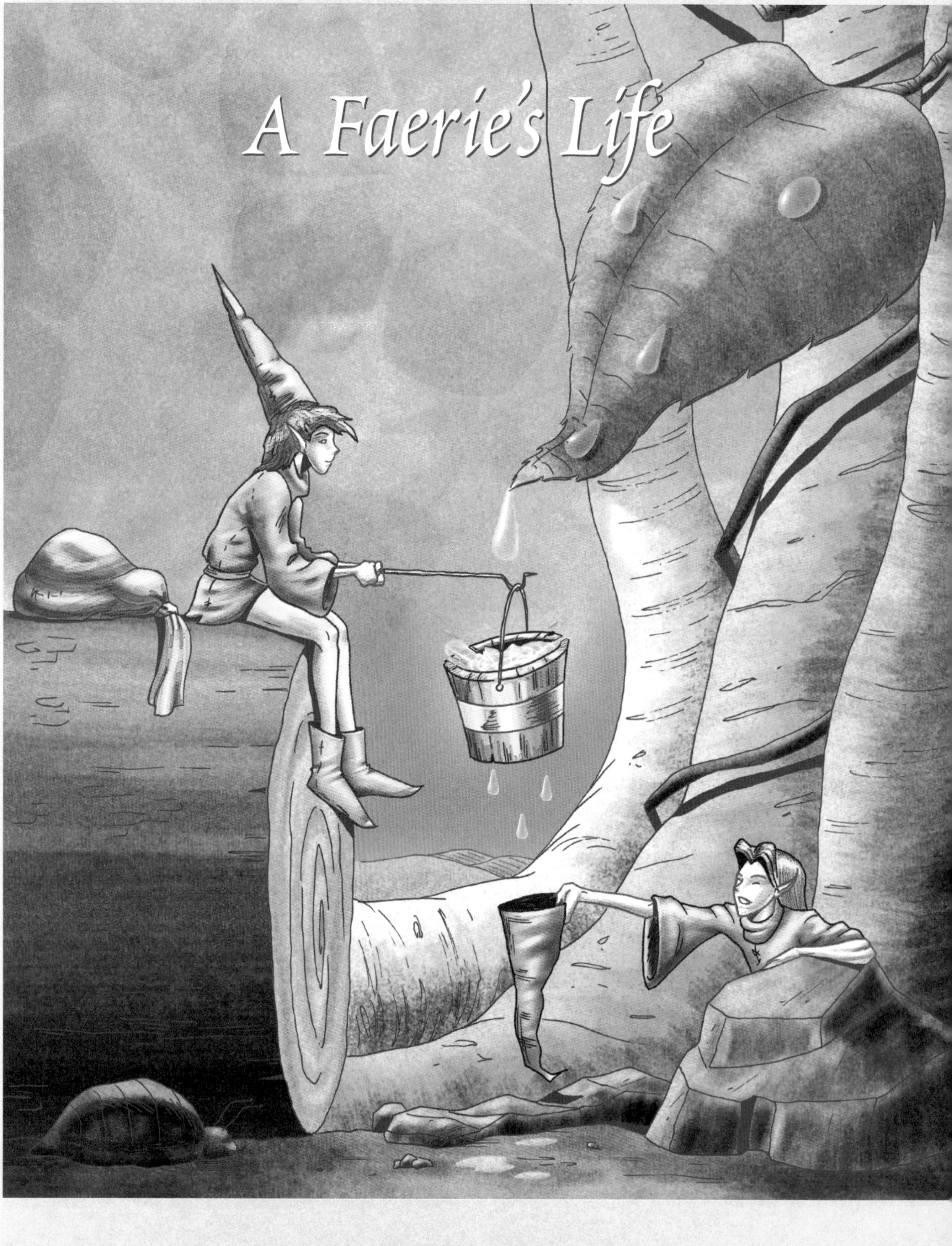

Faerie Families

Faeries have homes, families, and pets, just like us. Faerie families are so much fun to watch—they are just so loving and joyful. Baby faeries are as small as a fingernail and as light as the breeze. The babies learn how to spread their wings at an early age. They're flying long before they learn how to walk.

Childhood

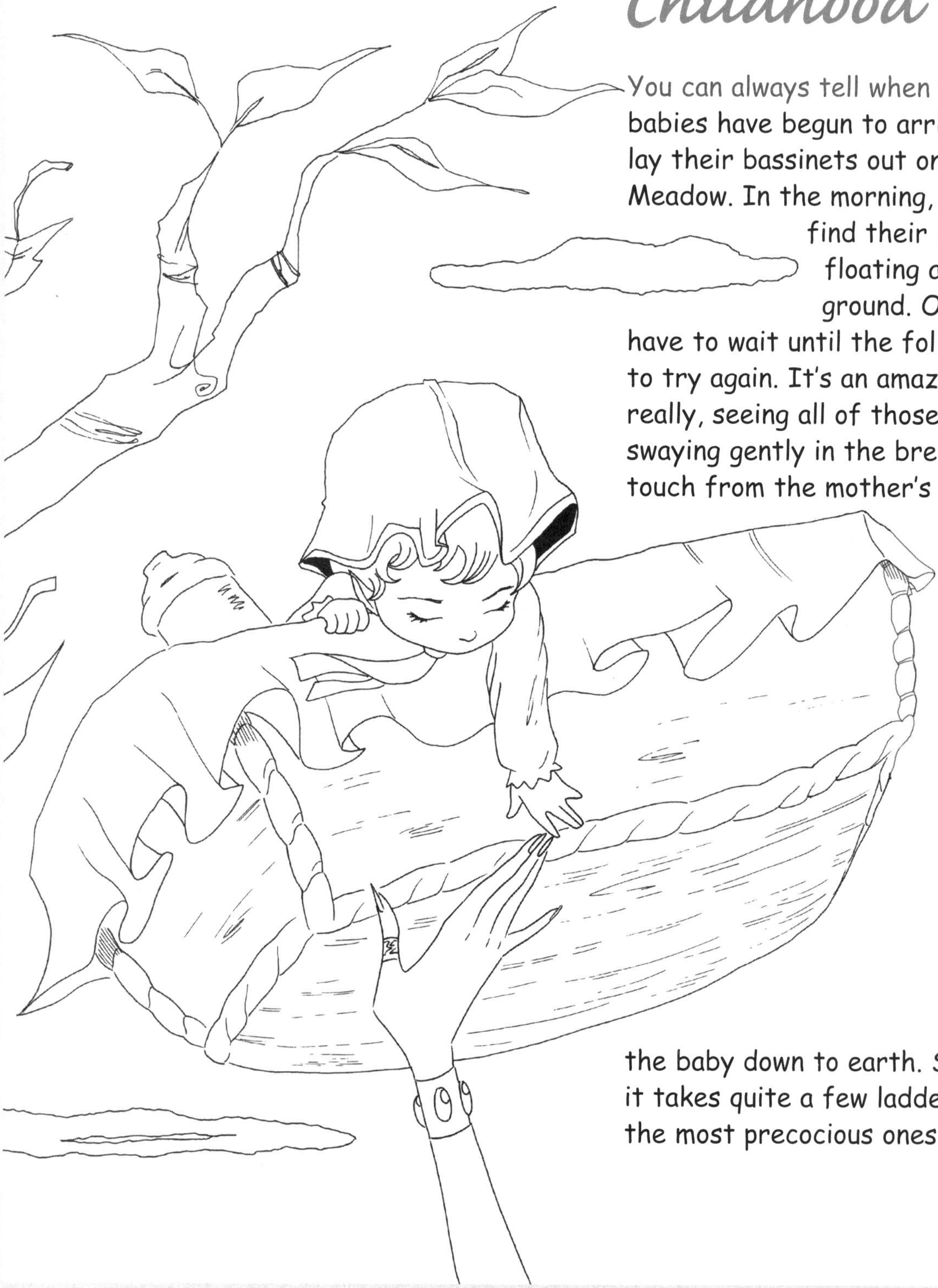

You can always tell when the new babies have begun to arrive. Mothers lay their bassinets out on the Great Meadow. In the morning, some will find their bassinets floating above the ground. Others will have to wait until the following year to try again. It's an amazing sight, really, seeing all of those bassinets swaying gently in the breeze. A touch from the mother's hand brings the baby down to earth. Sometimes, it takes quite a few ladders to reach the most precocious ones.

Making Magic

Faeries learn to influence the forces of nature at a very early age. Children are not permitted to practice magic, yet they've been known to sneak a spell or two when no grown-ups are watching. Note the rapture magic brings.

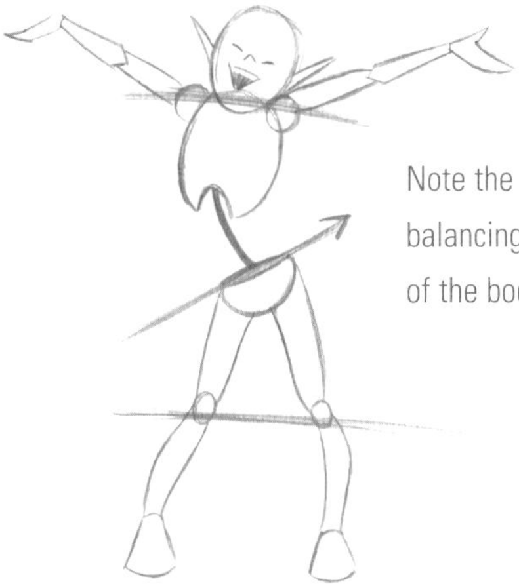

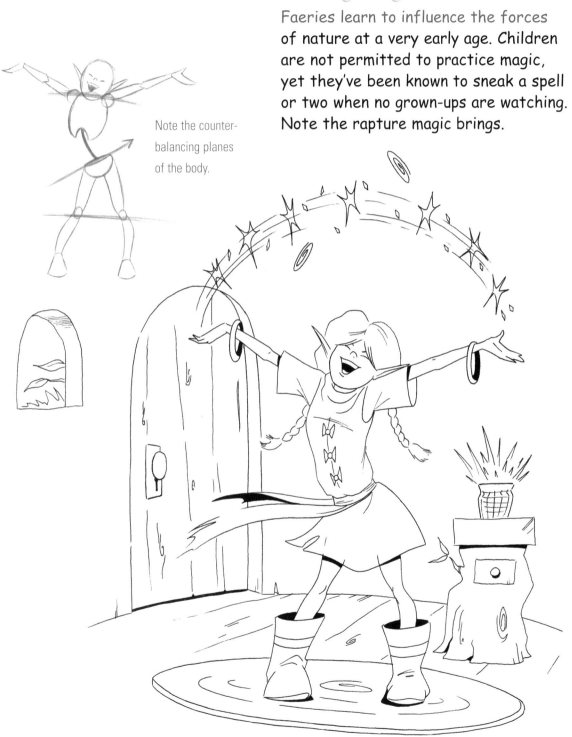

Note the counter-balancing planes of the body.

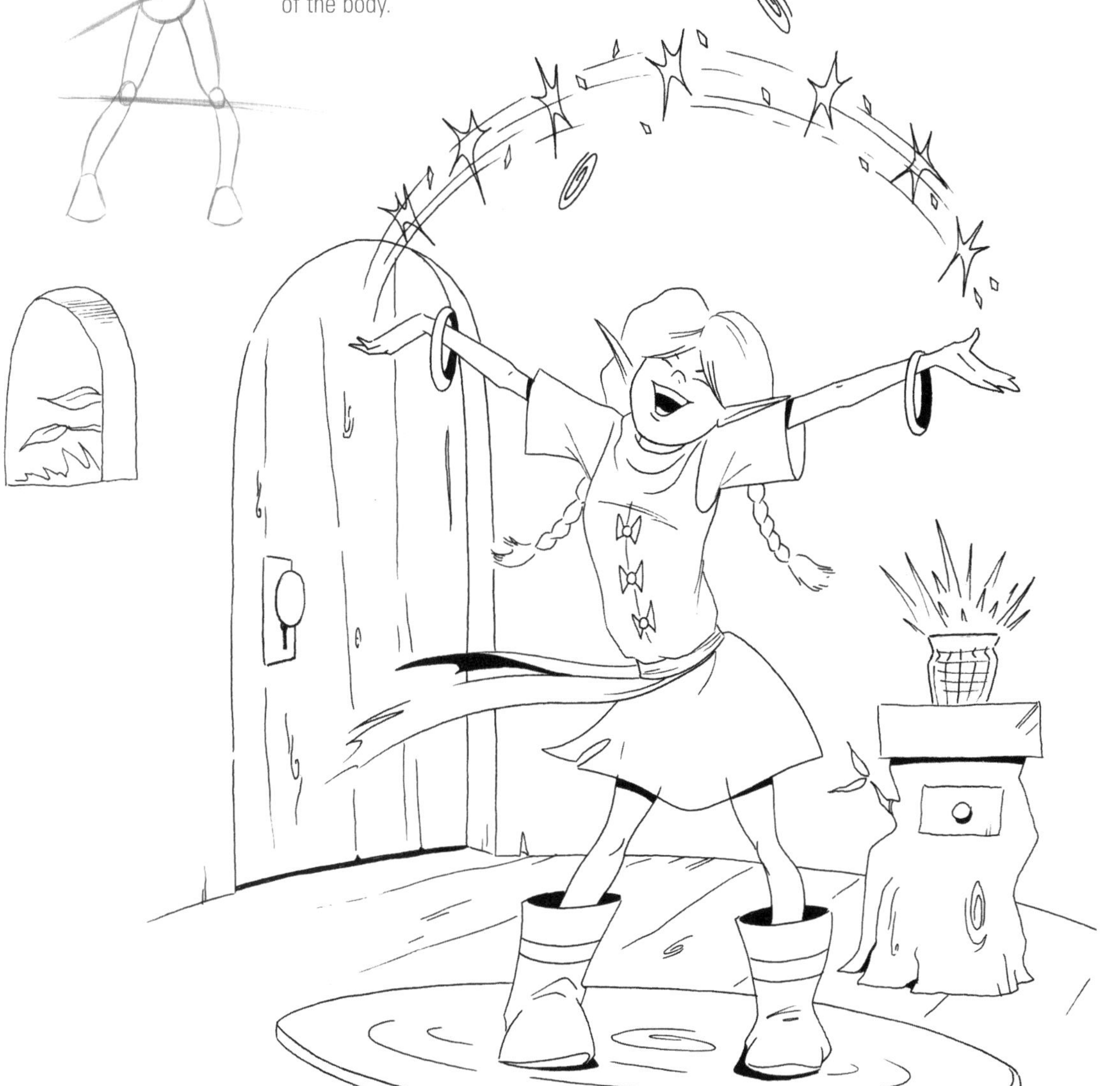

Courtship & Marriage

Faeries don't date the way humans do. Once that special connection is made, it is immediate, undeniable, and unwavering. When two faeries touch, their souls become one. Therefore, the first holding of the hands has profound meaning and passion.

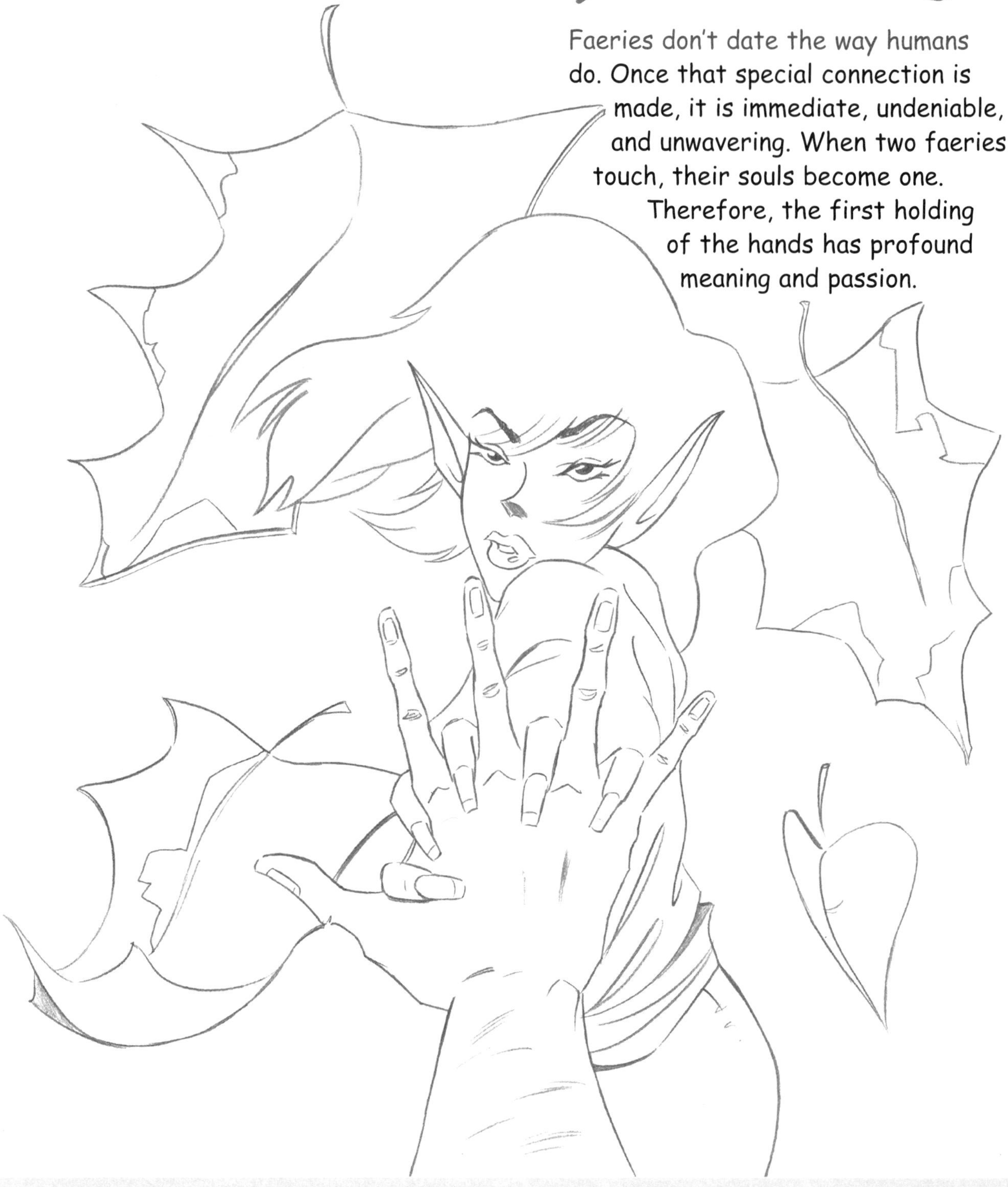

The Bond

There is no such thing as divorce among faerie couples. I have tried to explain the concept to them, but they just don't get it. They don't understand the idea at all. I like that about them.

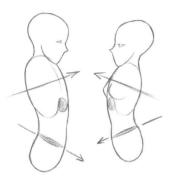

Note the angles at which the rib cage and pelvis diverge.

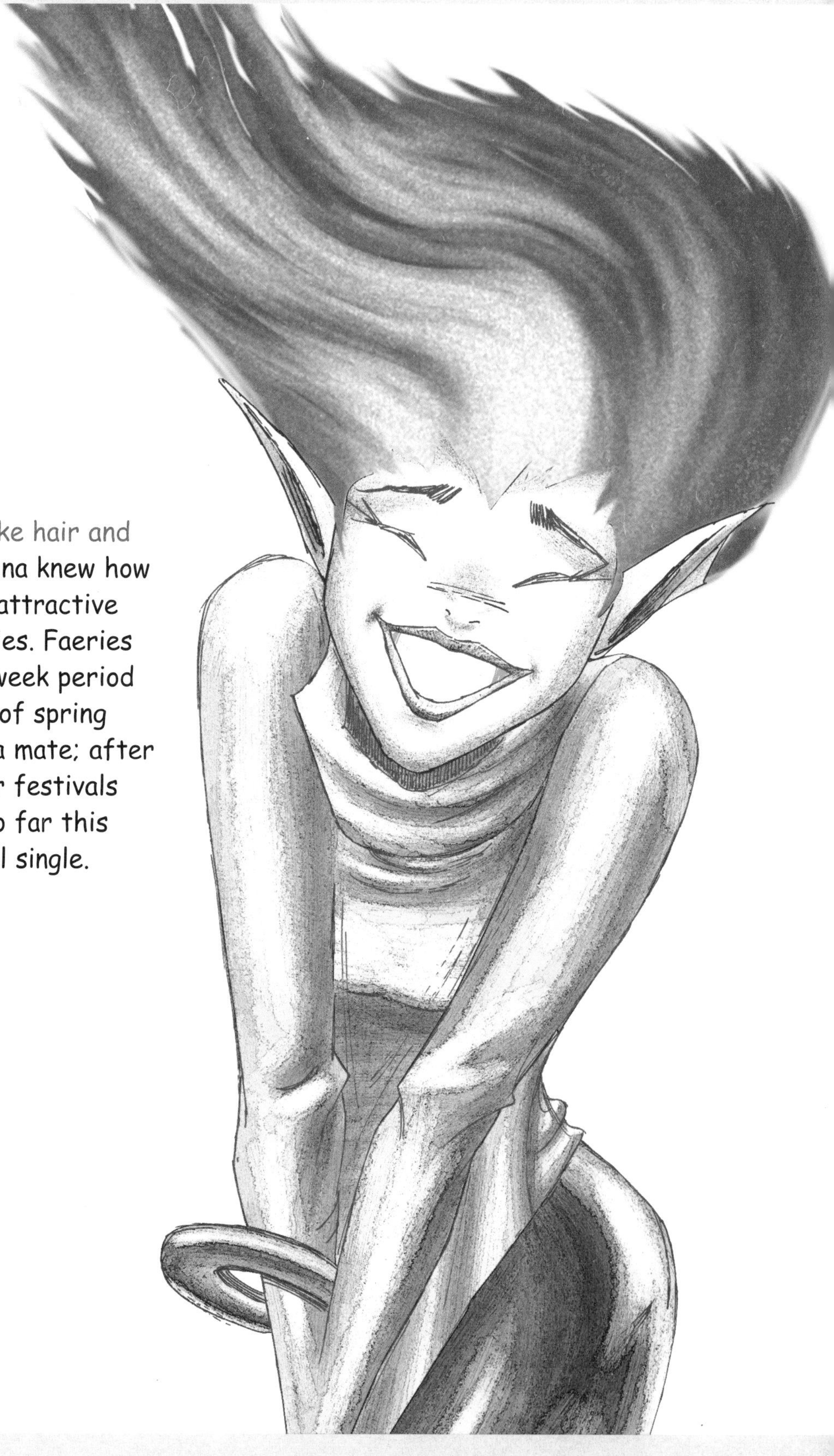

Nona

With her flamelike hair and inviting smile, Nona knew how to make herself attractive to the male faeries. Faeries only have a two-week period at the beginning of spring in which to find a mate; after that, the summer festivals intrude. Sadly, so far this year, Nona is still single.

Gilliam

Poor Gilliam. I saw her lose out to Nona many a season. She was interested in finding the right partner, and so went into many summers with no one. But love did eventually find her. She has been happily married for many years now.

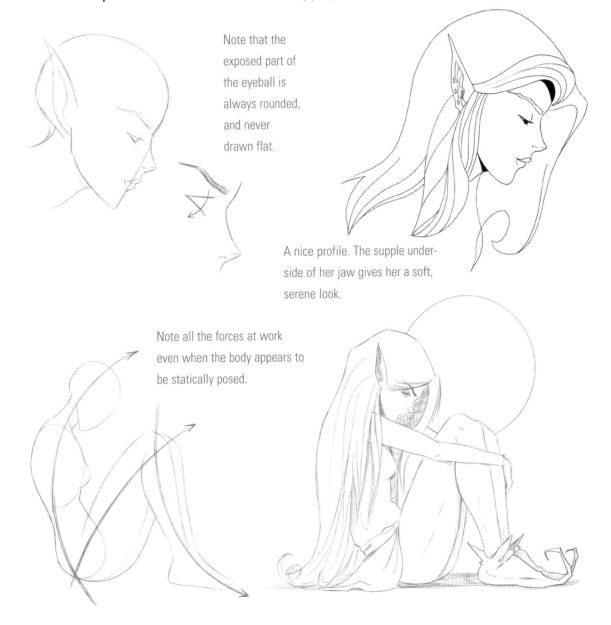

Note that the exposed part of the eyeball is always rounded, and never drawn flat.

A nice profile. The supple under-side of her jaw gives her a soft, serene look.

Note all the forces at work even when the body appears to be statically posed.

The Death of a Faerie

Faeries live for 600 years, whether or not they watch their diet. In fact, they live for such a long time that they often lose track of their age. Once they reach their prime (which is different for each faerie), they maintain that age for the duration of their lifespan. A faerie with little time left might marry a faerie with centuries, and both will be none the wiser. Then, one day—without warning—the life spirit will suddenly leave them, making each faerie's death an unexpected tragedy.

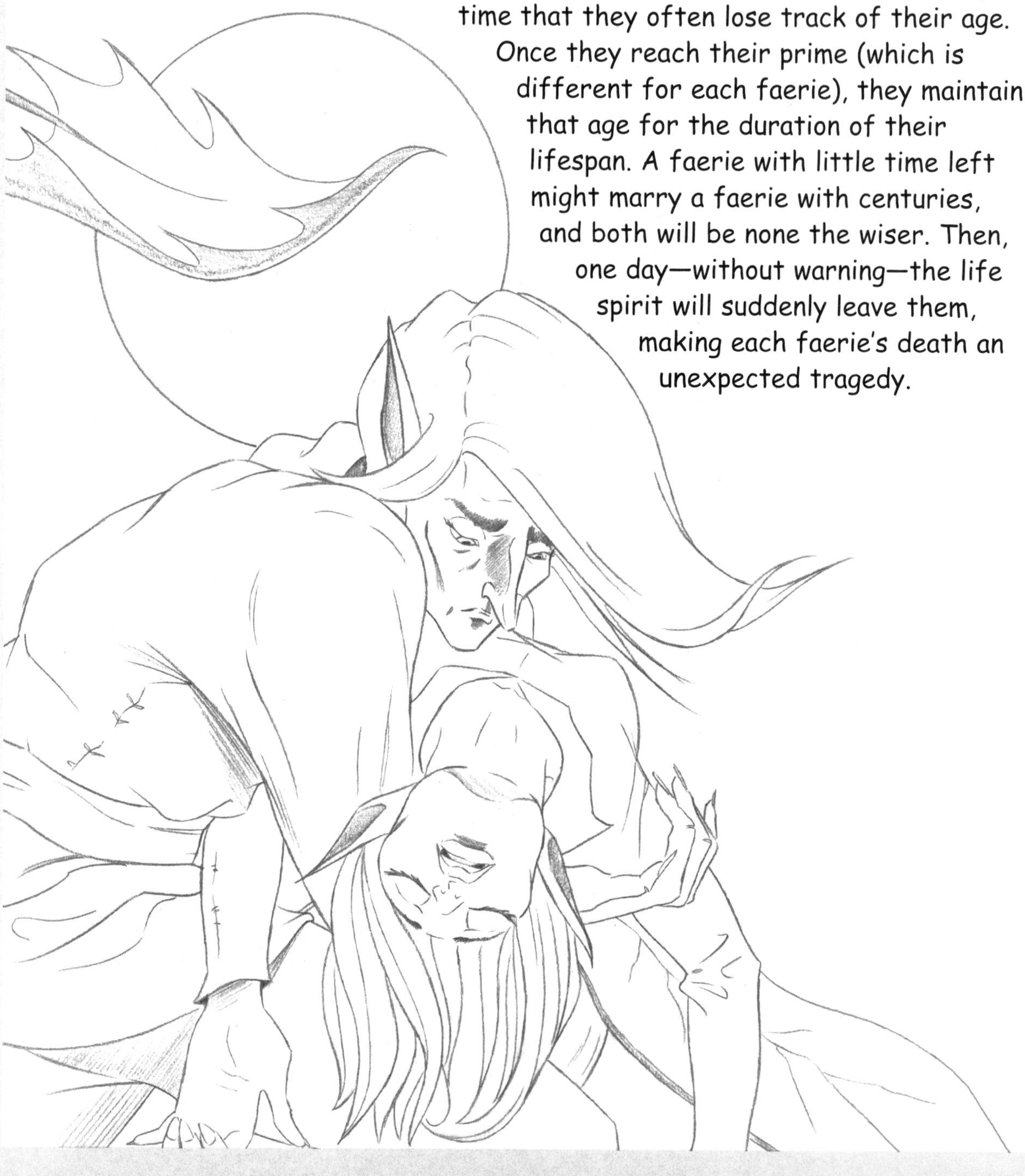

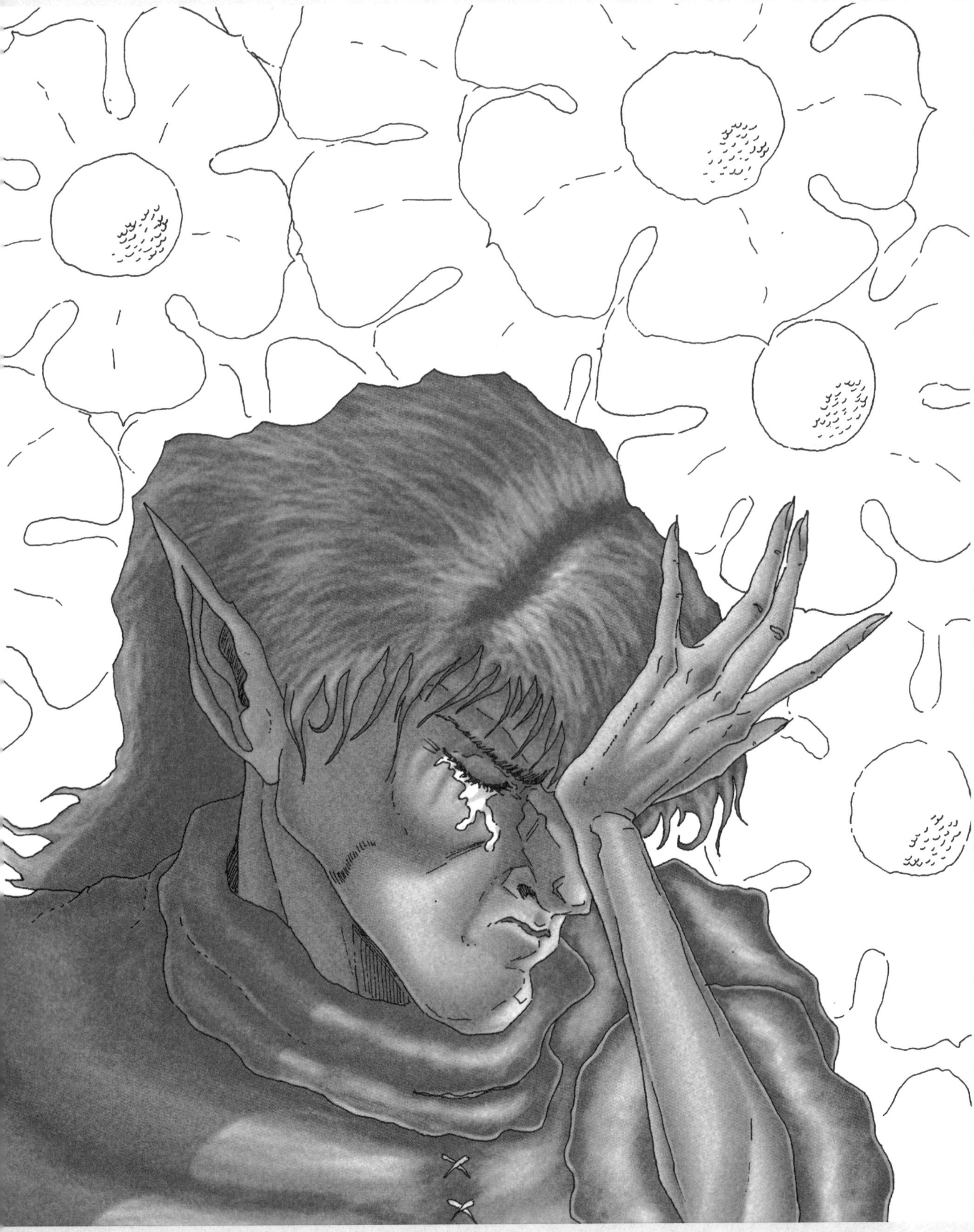

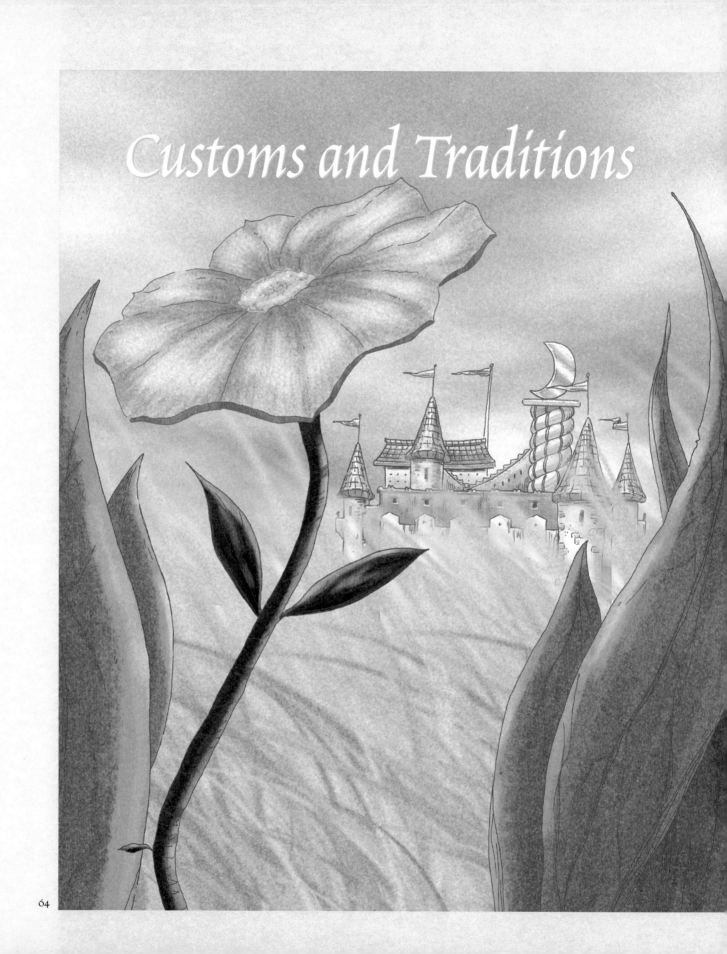

Customs and Traditions

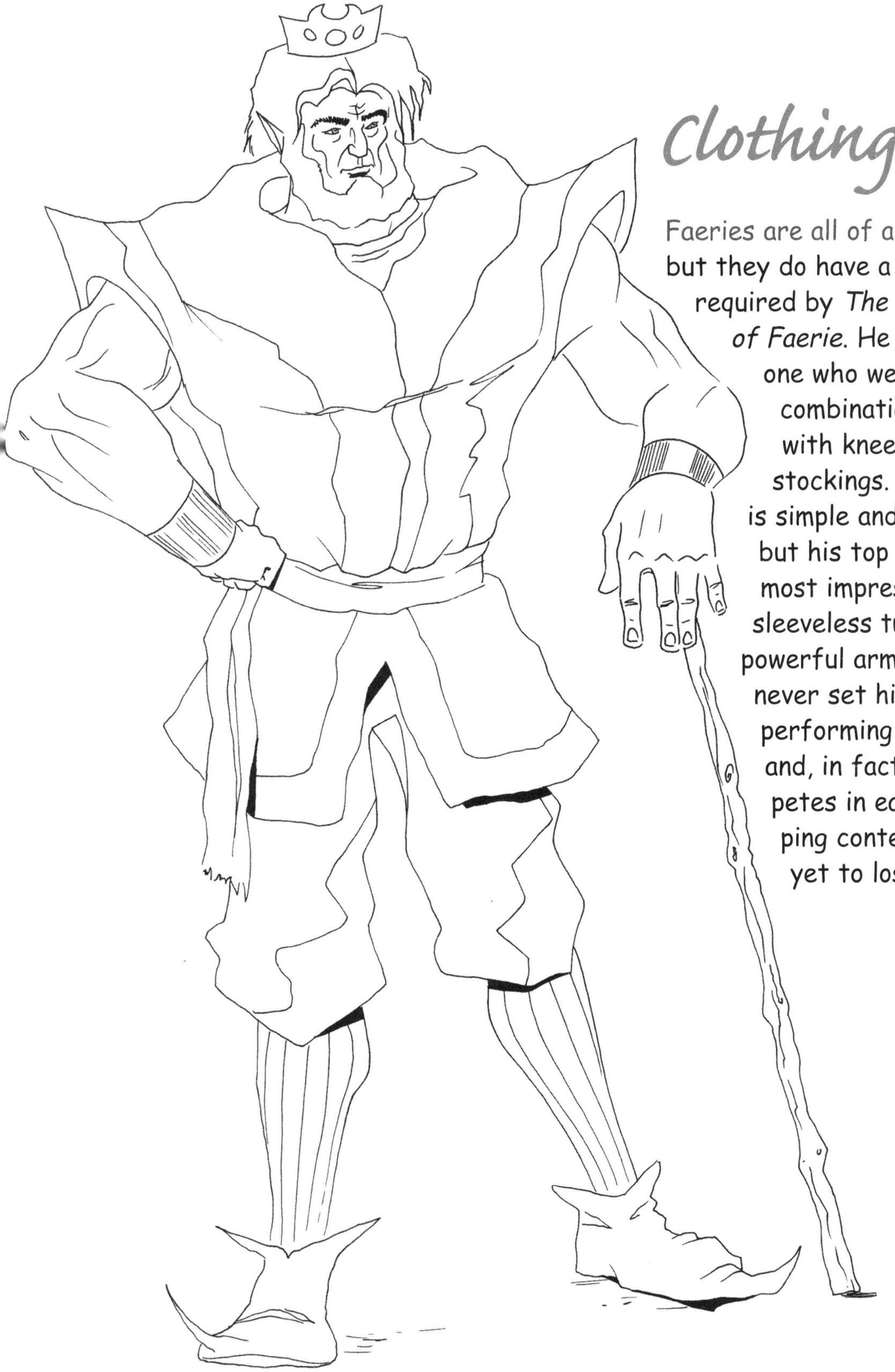

Clothing

Faeries are all of a common class, but they do have a king, as is required by *The Great Book of Faerie*. He is the only one who wears this combination of pants with knee-high stockings. His crown is simple and respectable, but his top garment is most impressive. The sleeveless tunic reveals his powerful arms. He has never set himself above performing manual labor and, in fact, eagerly competes in each fall's chopping contest—and has yet to lose the event!

Formal Attire

This lovely faerie will wear this dress but twice in her life. It was stitched together by many skilled hands and presented to her upon her twenty-first birthday. She will wear it at her wedding, with her beautiful wings unbound. And she will wear it when they lay her to rest, and then through eternity.

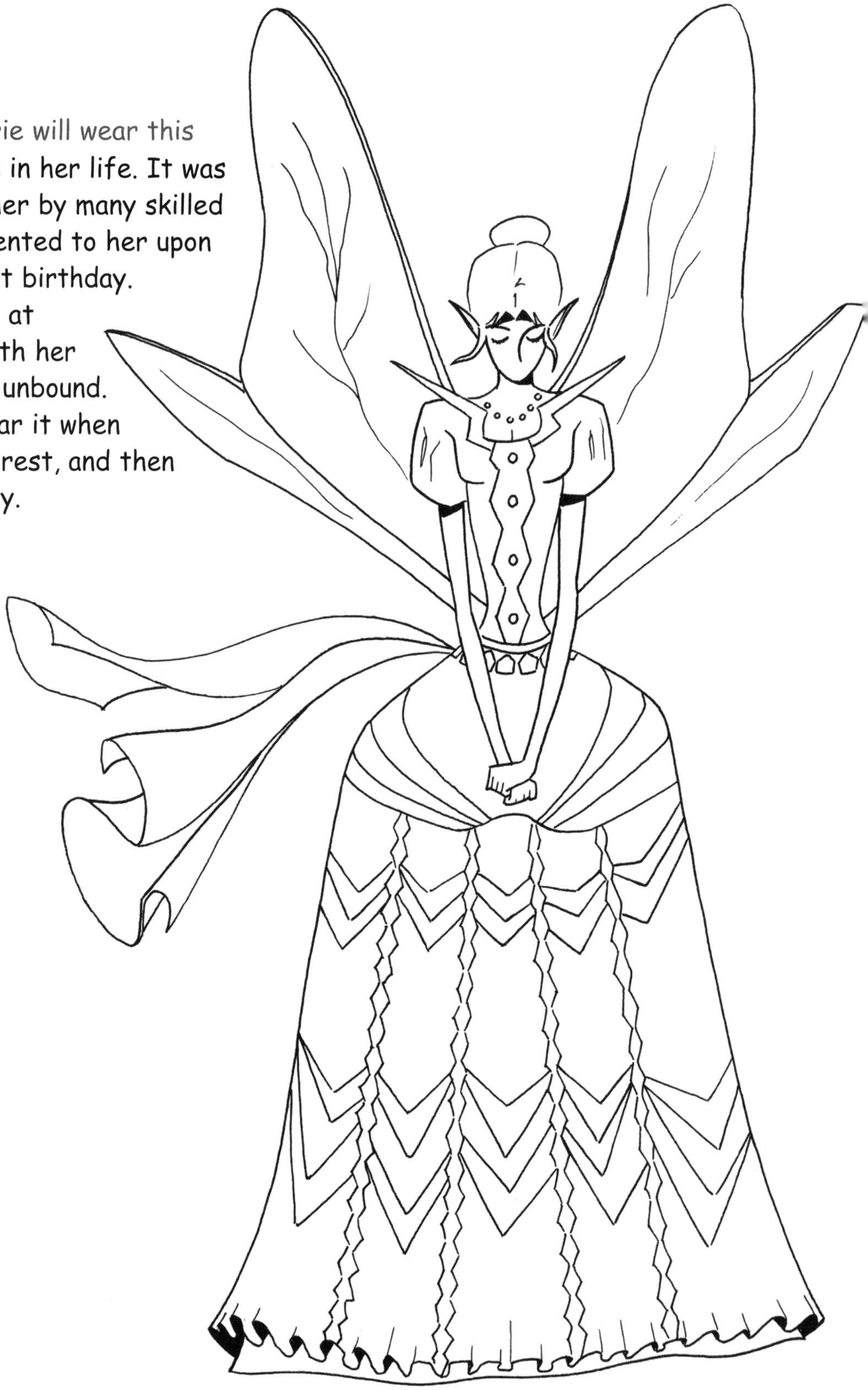

Daily Wear

Several layers of sturdy fabrics were stitched together to make this simple and pleasing outfit. Faerie dresses always remind me of those traditionally worn in Switzerland. Then again, it is most probable that the early Swiss were the first to discover the little beings and, therefore, were greatly influenced by them.

Bunching and Creasing

Faerie clothing is always worn loose, never tight. Because of this, the material reacts to the movement of the wearer.

When the arms are raised, the fabric creases at the arm/chest juncture. The turtleneck collar is pulled up, concealing the faerie's neck. The sleeves pull up, revealing the wrists.

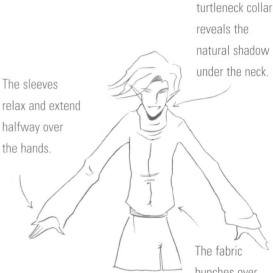

The sleeves relax and extend halfway over the hands.

When the arms are lowered, the turtleneck collar reveals the natural shadow under the neck.

The fabric bunches over the belt.

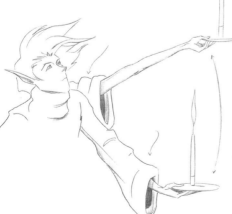

As the candle is lifted, the sleeve bunches up; lowered, the sleeve resumes its proper length.

The bent leg pulls on the material, requiring more fabric and, therefore, raising the pants, revealing the stocking.

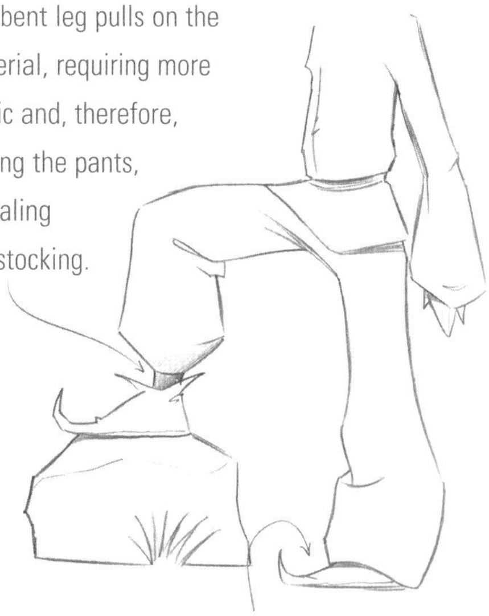

The straight leg allows the pants to cover the shoe, creasing the fabric near the bottom.

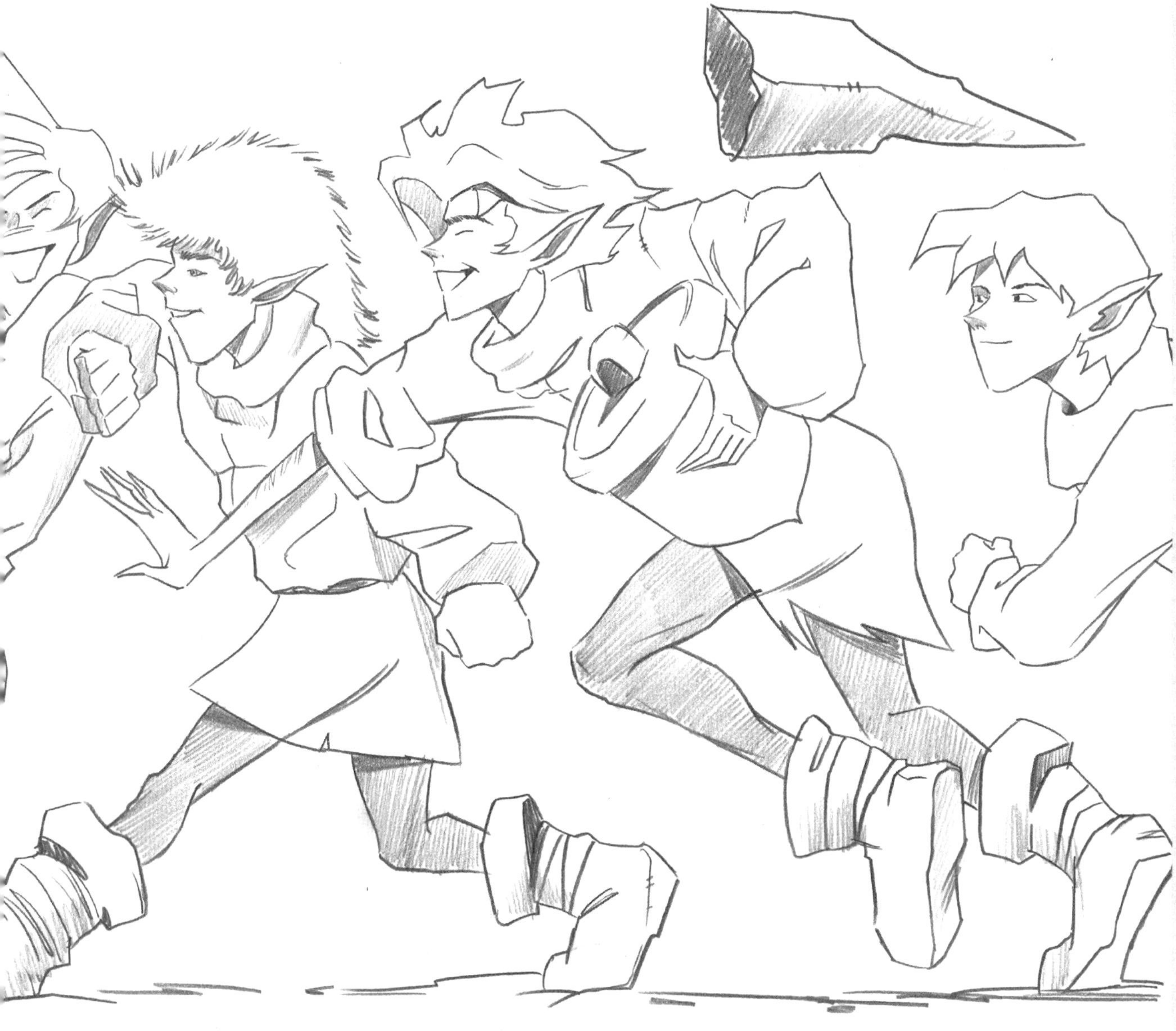

Houses & Dwellings

No two faerie homes are alike. Each is unique and special, made from salvaged wood, earth, stone, and metal. Most are just one room, with separate areas for eating, reading, and sleeping. Of course, being so tiny in size, faeries can find shelter pretty easily in a pinch.

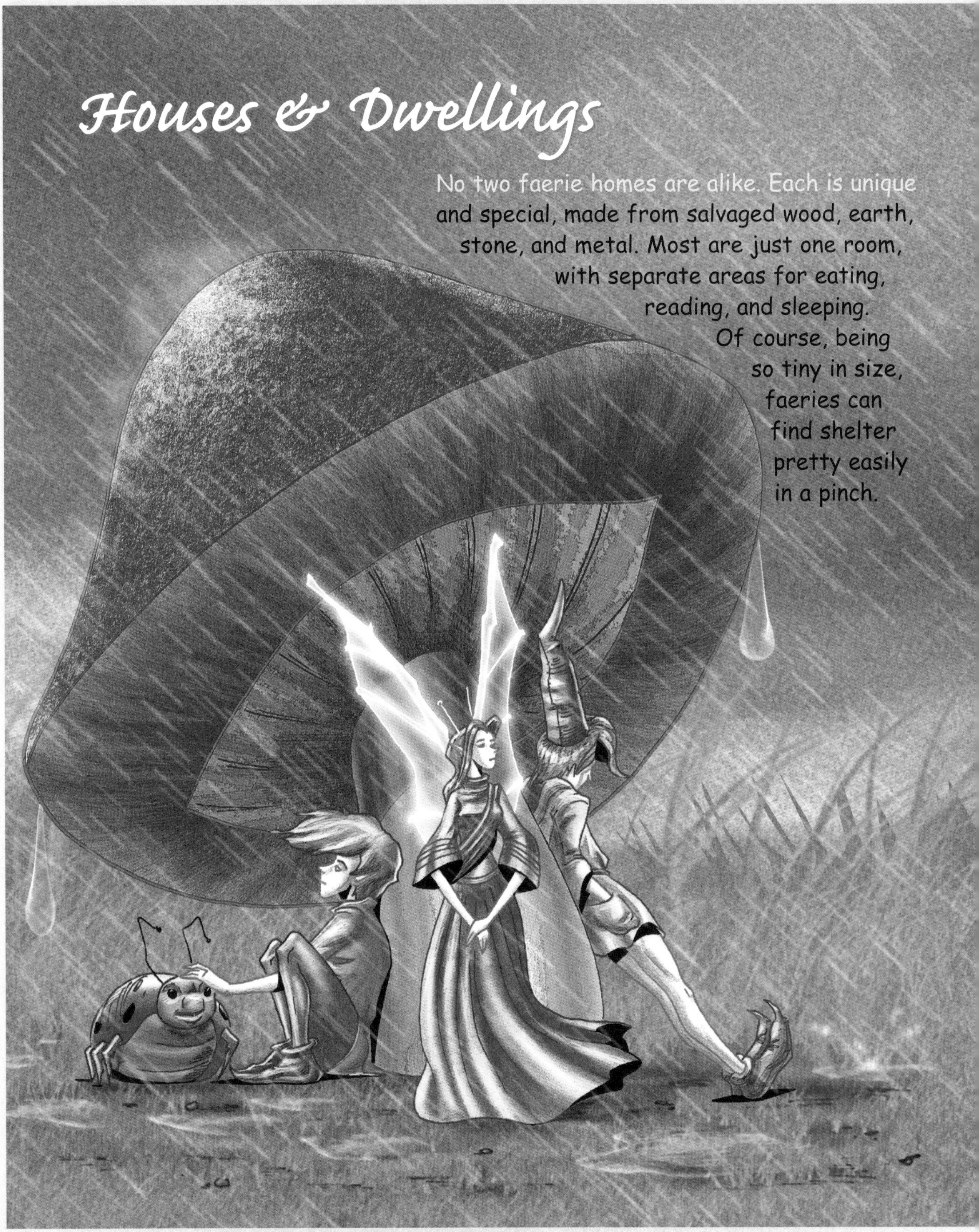

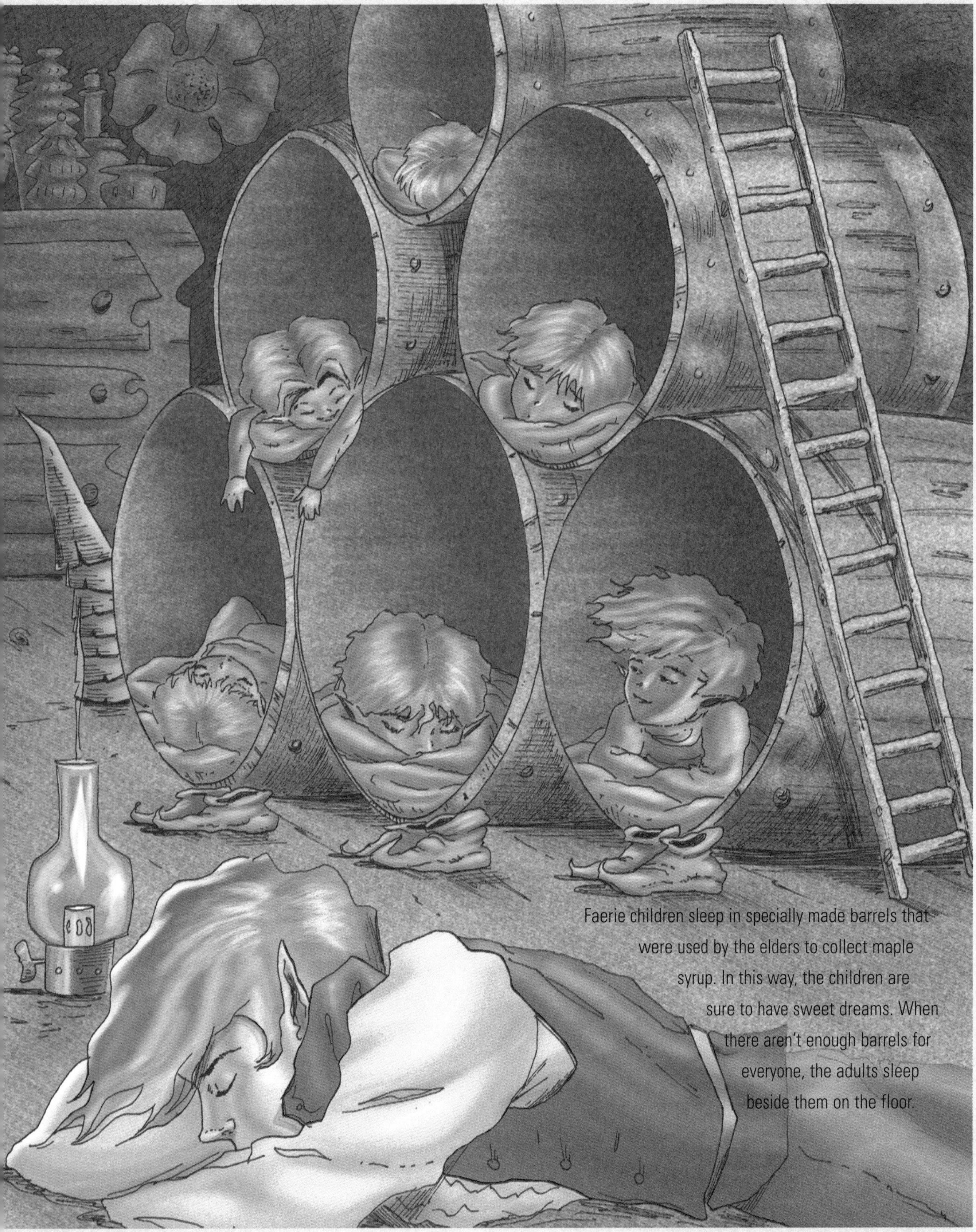

Faerie children sleep in specially made barrels that were used by the elders to collect maple syrup. In this way, the children are sure to have sweet dreams. When there aren't enough barrels for everyone, the adults sleep beside them on the floor.

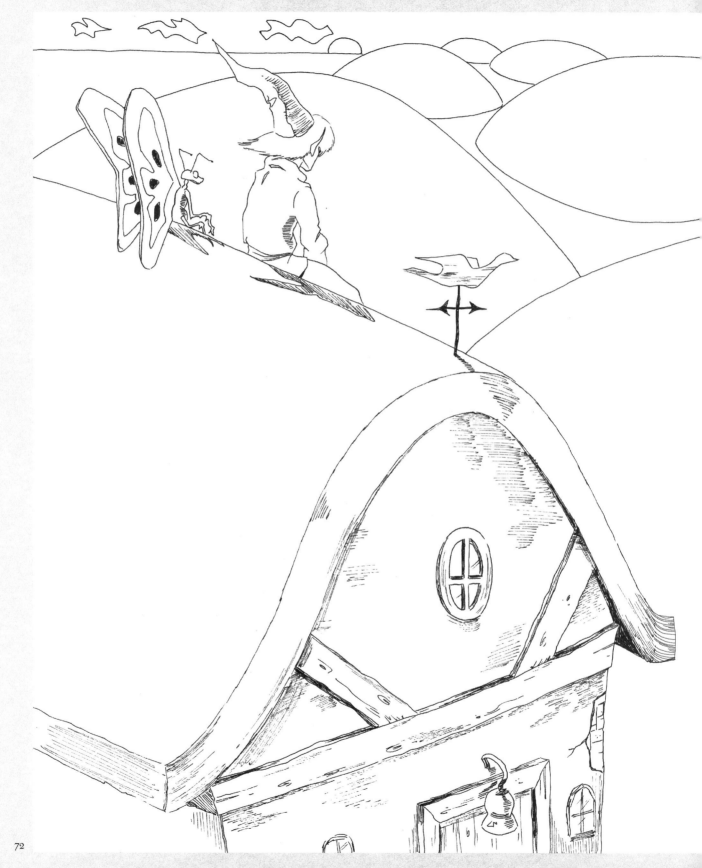

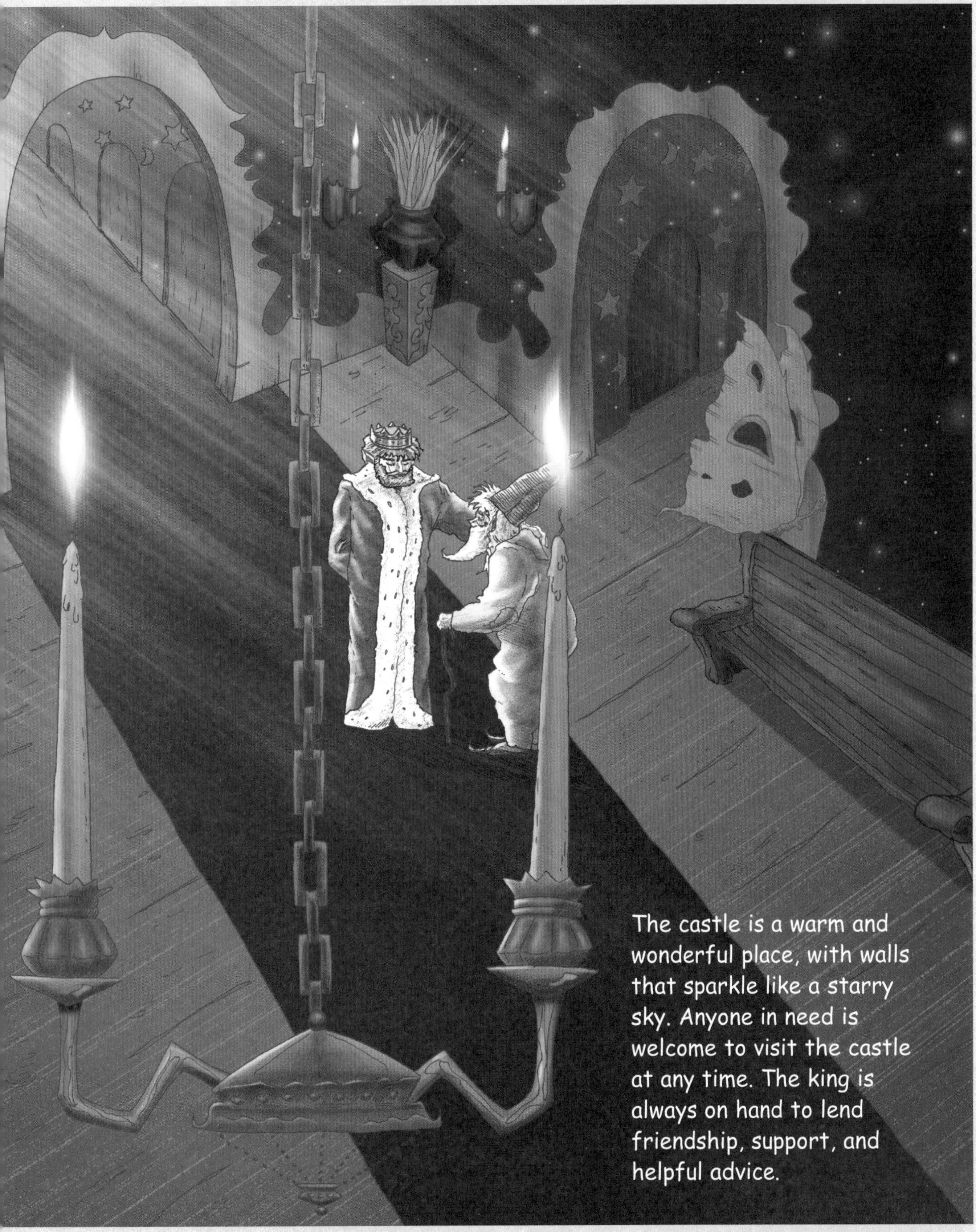

The castle is a warm and wonderful place, with walls that sparkle like a starry sky. Anyone in need is welcome to visit the castle at any time. The king is always on hand to lend friendship, support, and helpful advice.

Keeper of the Fire

One of the unenviable, but necessary, chores in the castle is maintaining the heat. It takes a great deal of sweat to feed the fire. Each faerie has his own technique. This fellow has fine-tuned his motion into a sweeping action. I enjoyed the silhouette that he cut, so I sketched him performing his task.

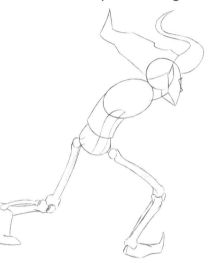

As a general rule, the more energy a task requires, the farther apart the legs are positioned.

For complex leg positions, it's often helpful to sketch out the bones first.

For the general thrust of the pose, I use what's called a "line of action," upon which I build the frame.

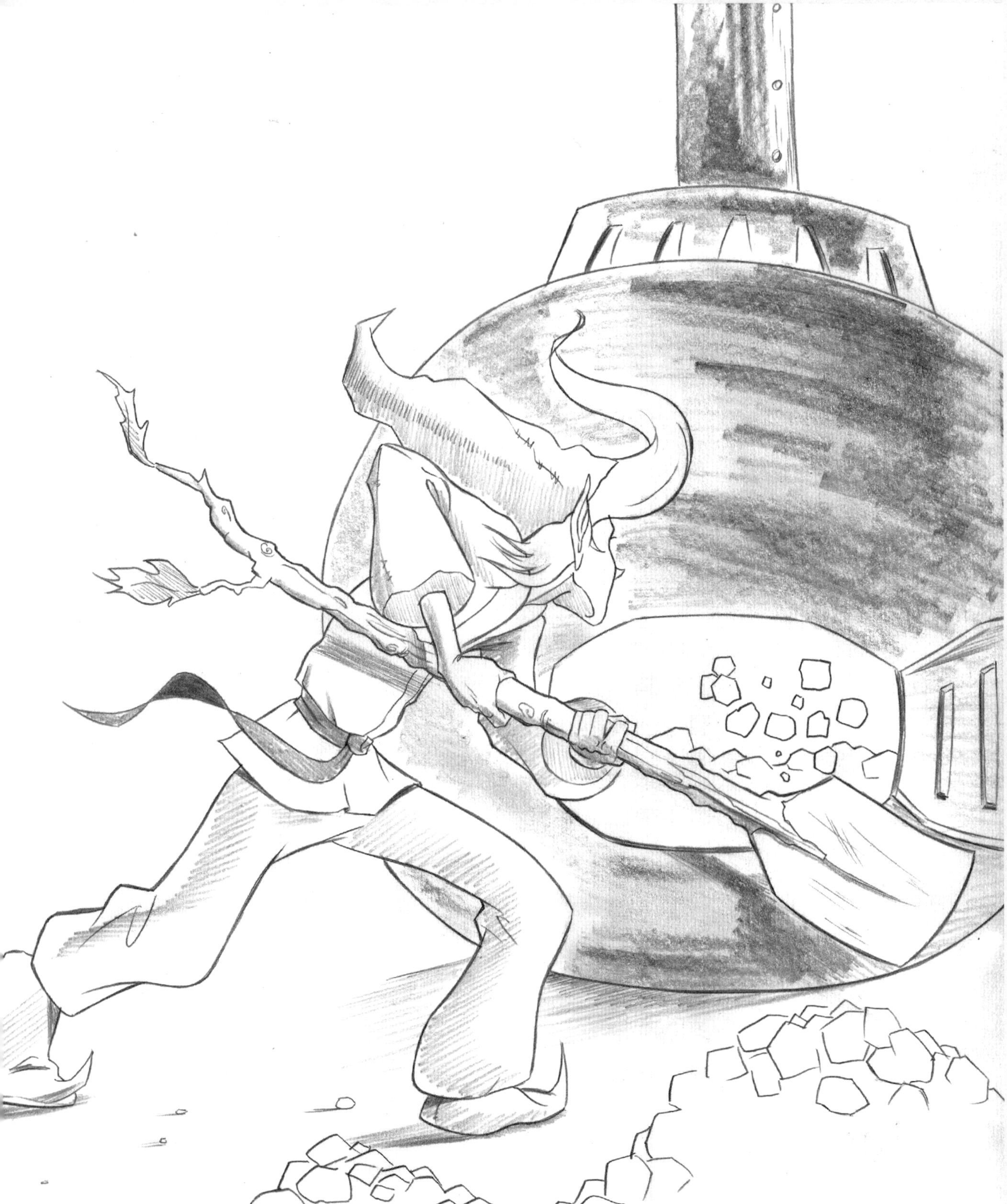

A Delicious Nap Afterward

After all of the hard work stoking the fire, a nice long nap is welcome and well deserved. Faeries never overwork or overplay, but instead balance their work time with plenty of rest. I think humans could learn a lot from faeries.

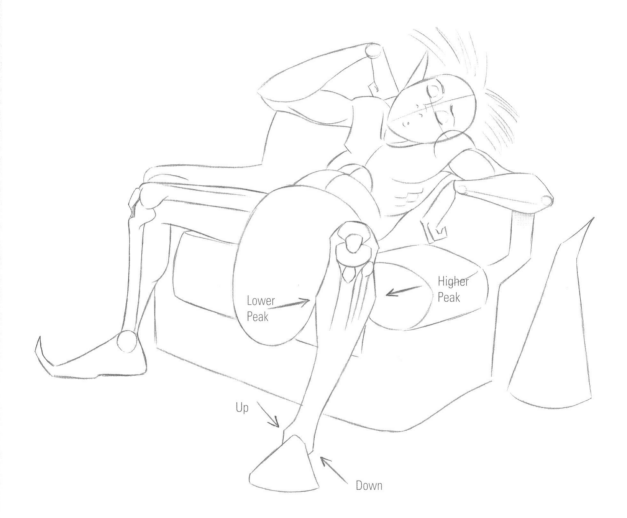

Lower Peak

Higher Peak

Up

Down

Since there is very little fat on faeries, the shape of their muscles must be clearly articulated. The calf muscle makes a good example. The muscle on the outer calf should always be drawn higher than the one on the inner calf. Conversely, the anklebone on the inside of the leg is always higher than the anklebone on the outside of the leg. In this regard, the anatomy of faeries and humans is identical.

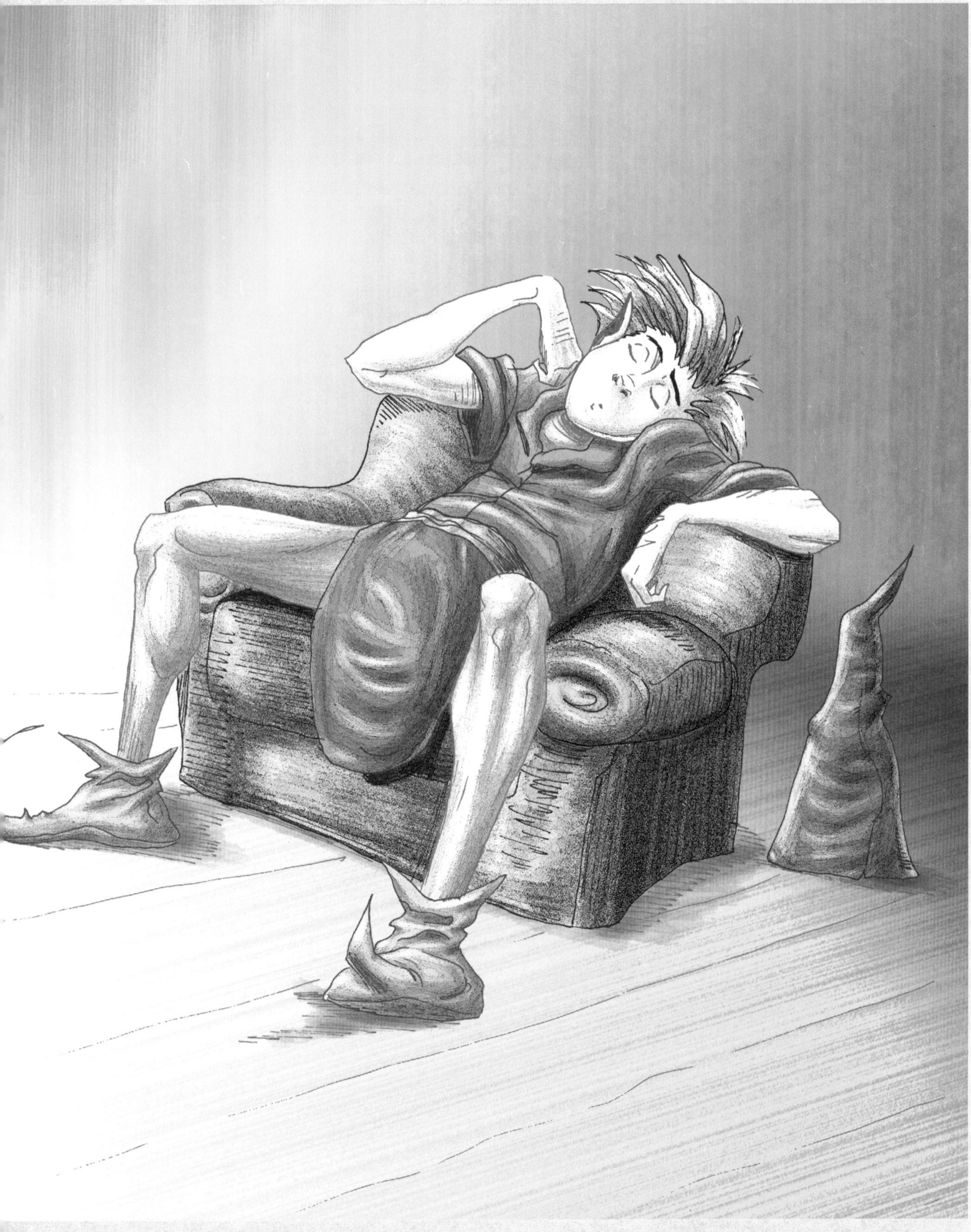

The Feast

Every year, in honor of nature's fruitful harvest, the faeries hold a special feast in the Great Hall of the castle. Every faerie in the village partakes in the preparations, either gathering and preparing the food, or decorating the hall for the big event.

Gathering

Here in New England, we go to the orchards for apple picking every September and October, so I know what a treat this time of year can be. Whereas I'll bring home a bucket of apples, faeries, being such small creatures, need far less. They search for just the right berry—the perfect berry. And when one of them has found it, the entire village rejoices.

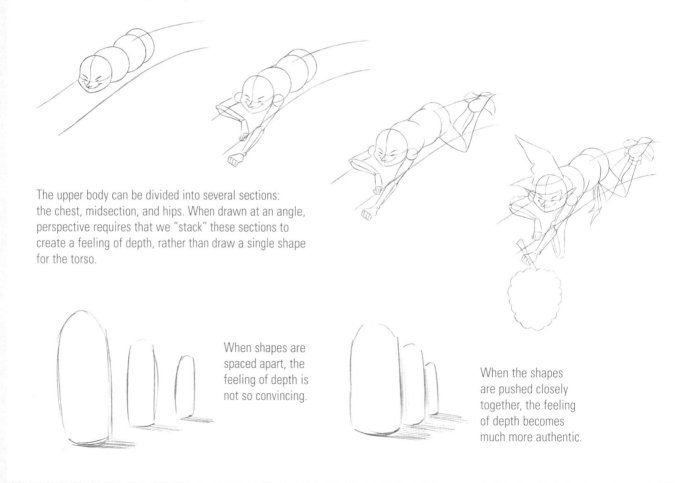

The upper body can be divided into several sections: the chest, midsection, and hips. When drawn at an angle, perspective requires that we "stack" these sections to create a feeling of depth, rather than draw a single shape for the torso.

When shapes are spaced apart, the feeling of depth is not so convincing.

When the shapes are pushed closely together, the feeling of depth becomes much more authentic.

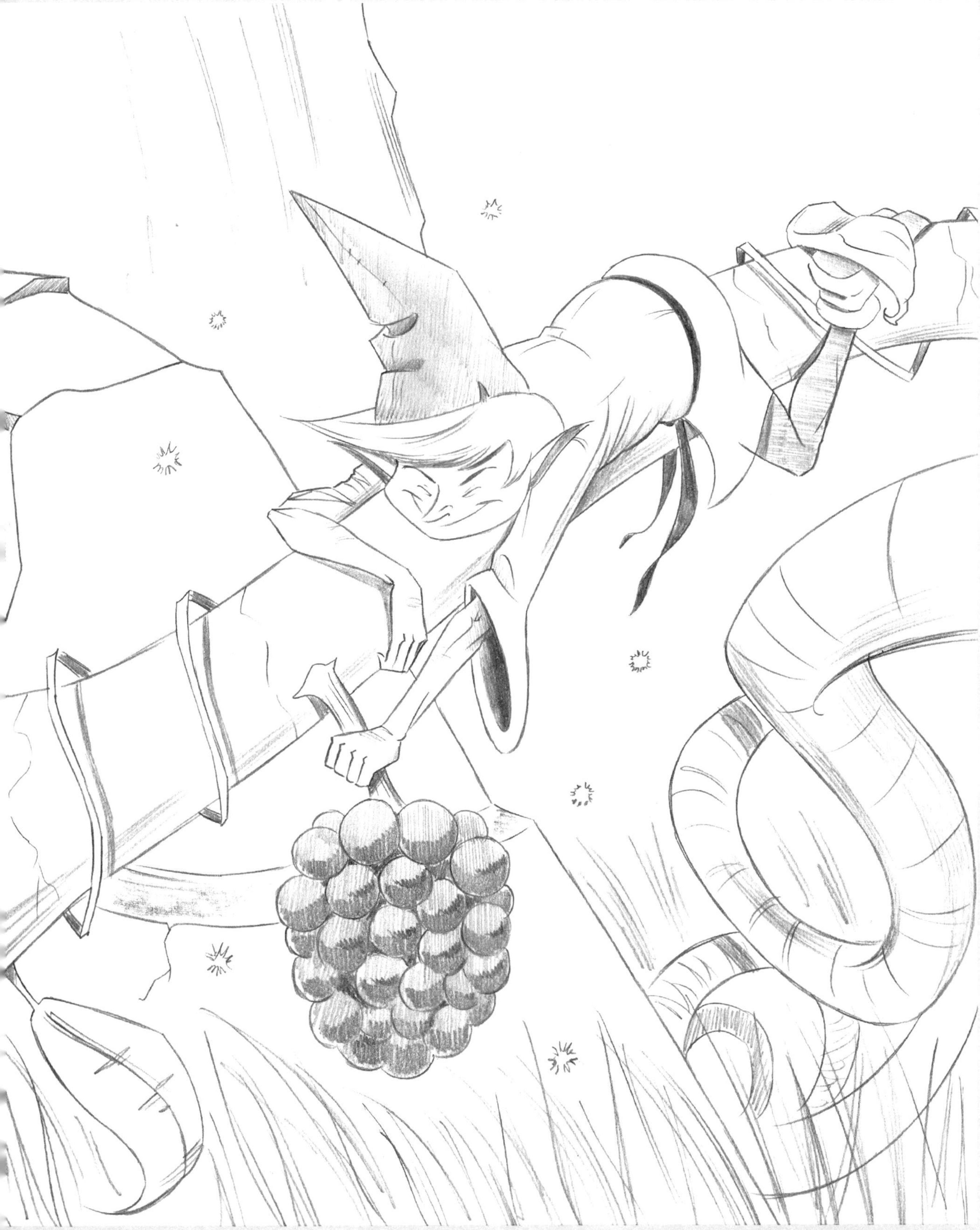

Times of Plenty

After the harvest, when food overflows at supper tables, is a wonderful time in the kingdom. It's a celebration, with bellies full of tasty morsels and an innate feeling that life is good.

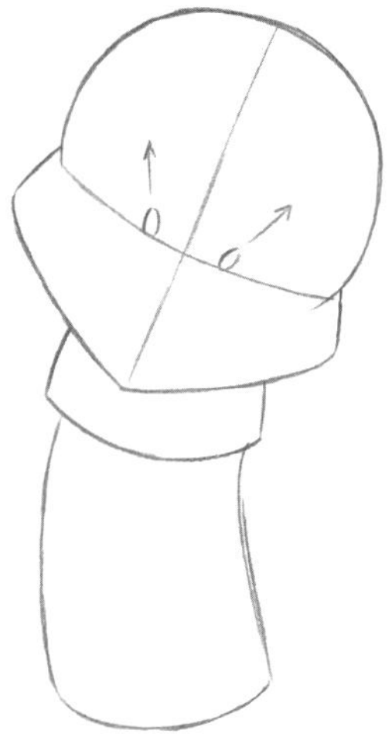

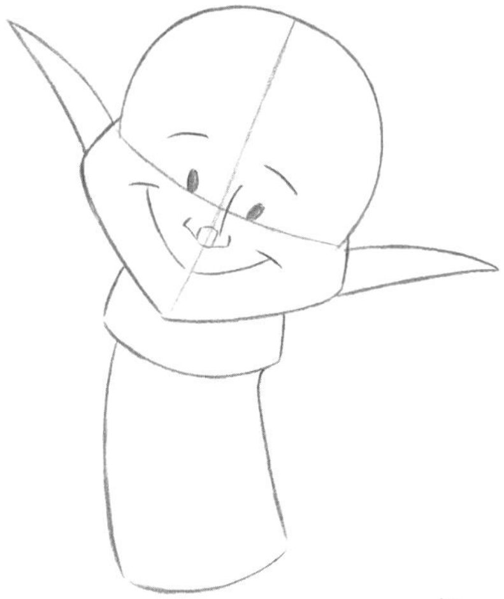

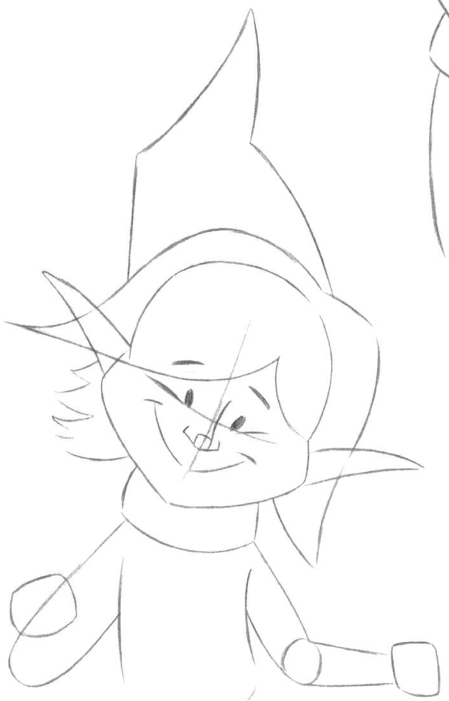

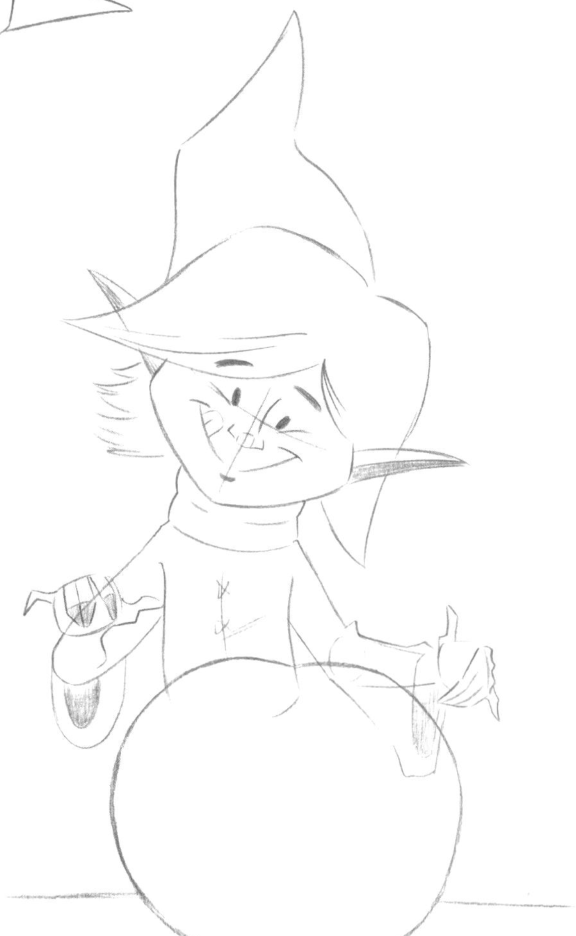

Allerick was a favorite faerie of mine. His small, coal-black eyes would glimmer whenever he smiled—which was all of the time. A particularly small faerie (yes, I know they are all small, but there are a few tallish faeries—and Allerick was not one of them), Allerick had a big spirit, and close friends numbering in the hundreds.

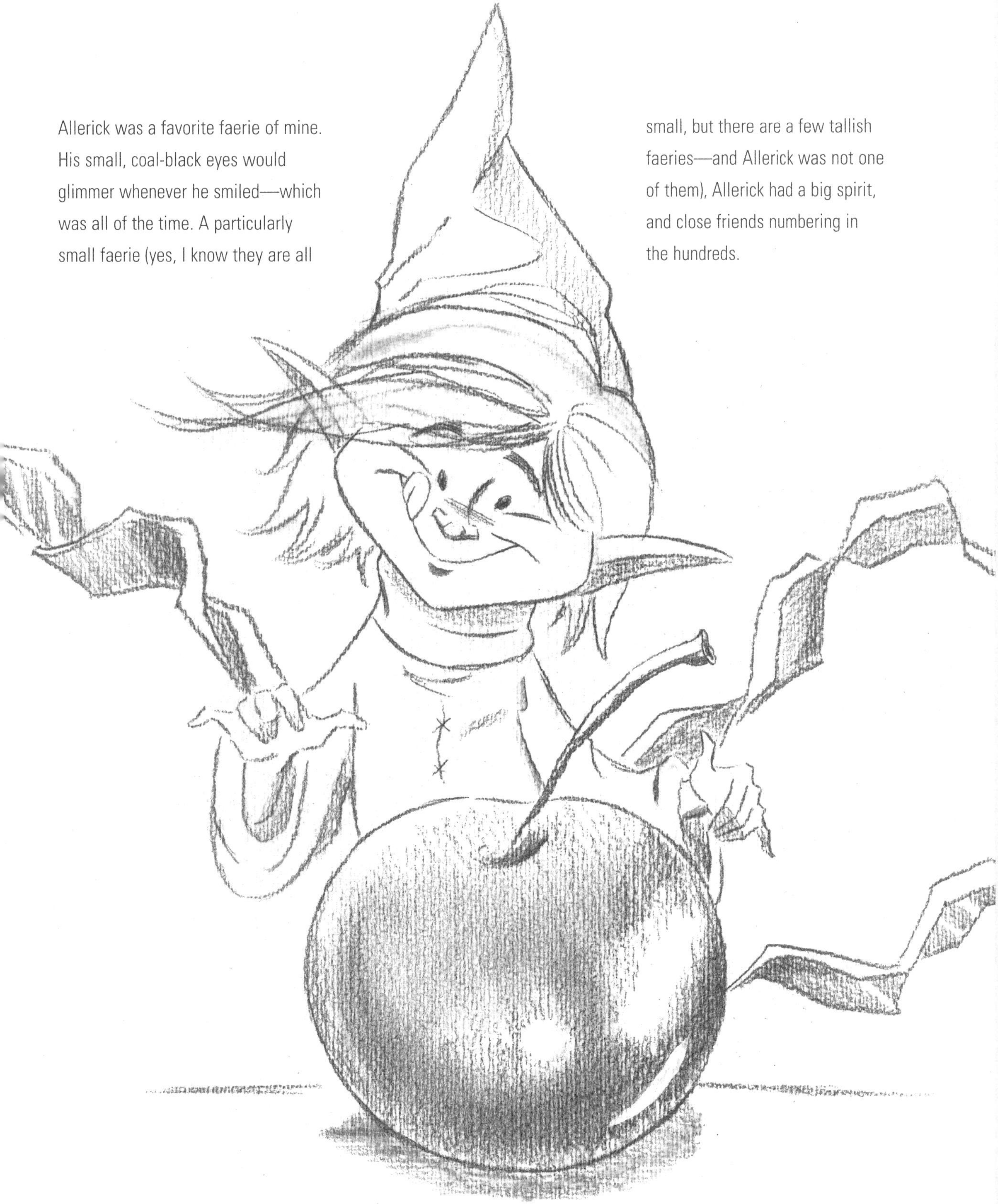

Walking Happy

When faeries are especially happy, they shift into this amusing, little gate: they walk with their arms and legs on each side moving in tandem, rather than one forward and one back, as we humans do. This gives them an extra little bounce in their stride. You'll almost always see them walk like this on their way home from the harvest.

Note the pleasing curve of the spine, as their posture reflects the buoyancy of their spirit.

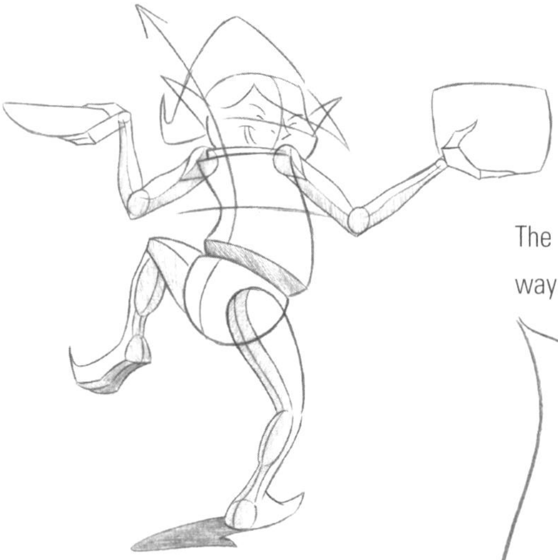

The leg and arm on the same side move forward as a pair, unlike the way humans walk.

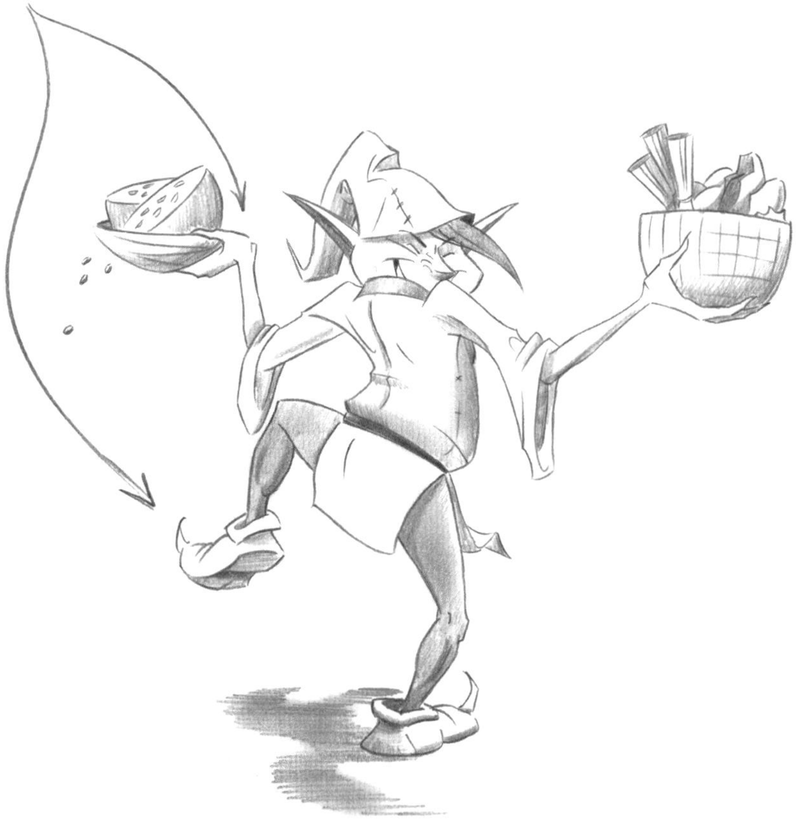

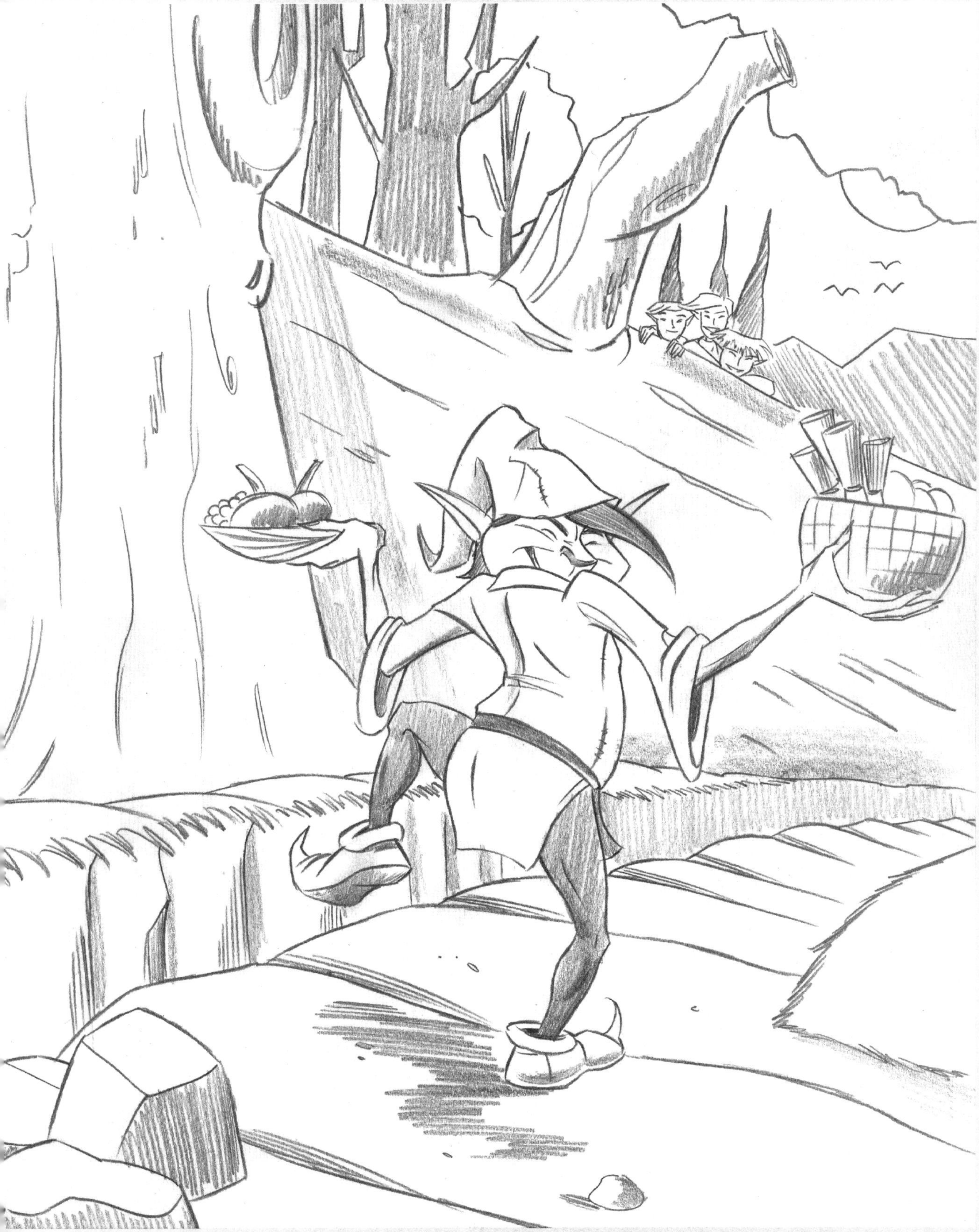

Preparing for the Feast

Once all the food has been gathered, the cooking begins. Many delicious entrees are prepared. Everyone wants to be a taster, but few want to be the cook. Some things never change, no matter how big or tiny you are.

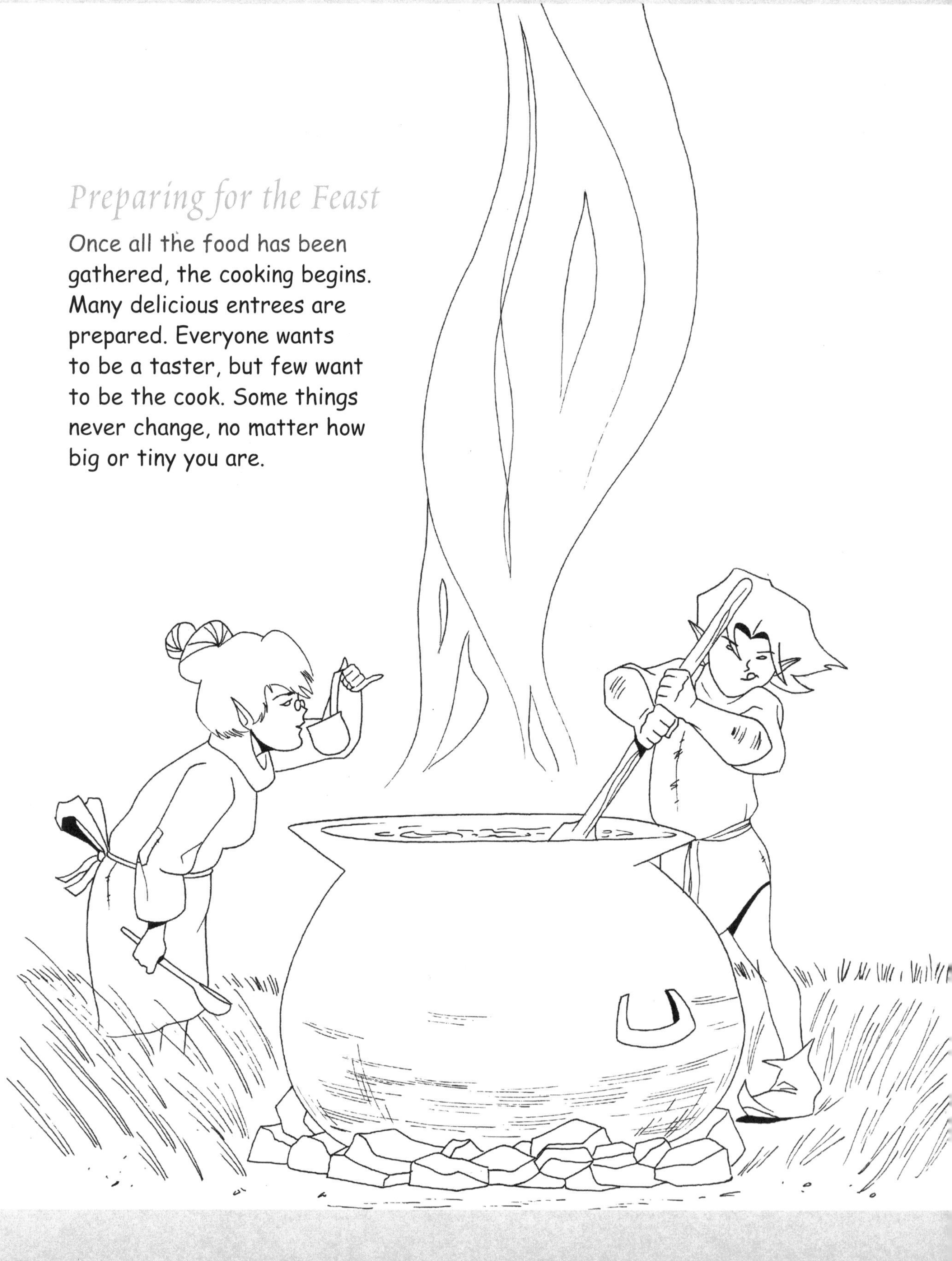

Anticipation

Aroma wafts through the Great Hall as the procession of treats and comestibles makes its way to the dining tables. Pies and tarts, honey-dipped biscuits and pastries, nectars, cheeses, fruits, seeds, and sweet soups...these are among the savory delights.

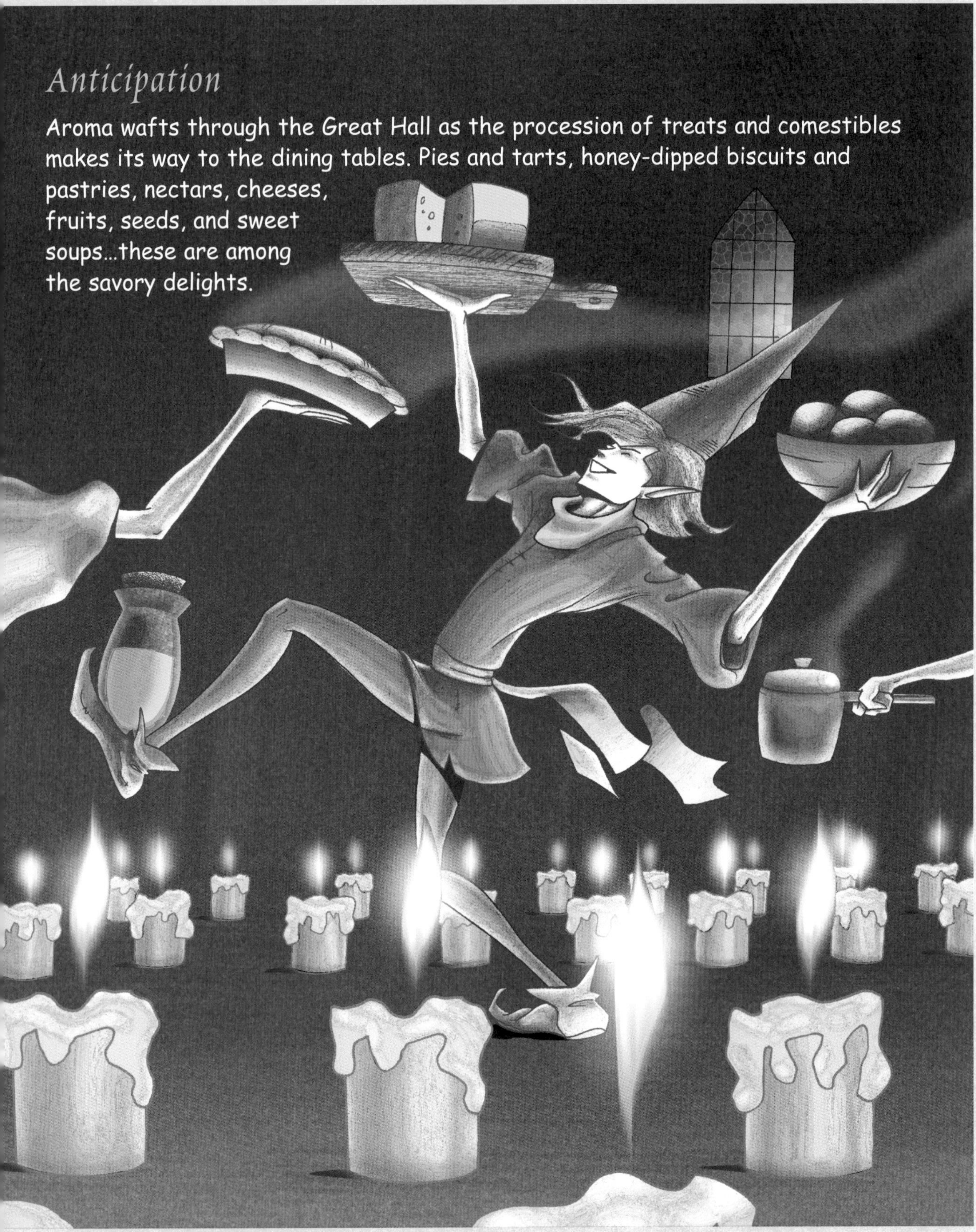

The King

After the feast, the king retreats to the Throne Room, where he holds court. Guests bring him small gifts of thanks, and he in turn presents them with books and other such treasures. The king rules with a gentle and loving hand, and is much beloved throughout the kingdom.

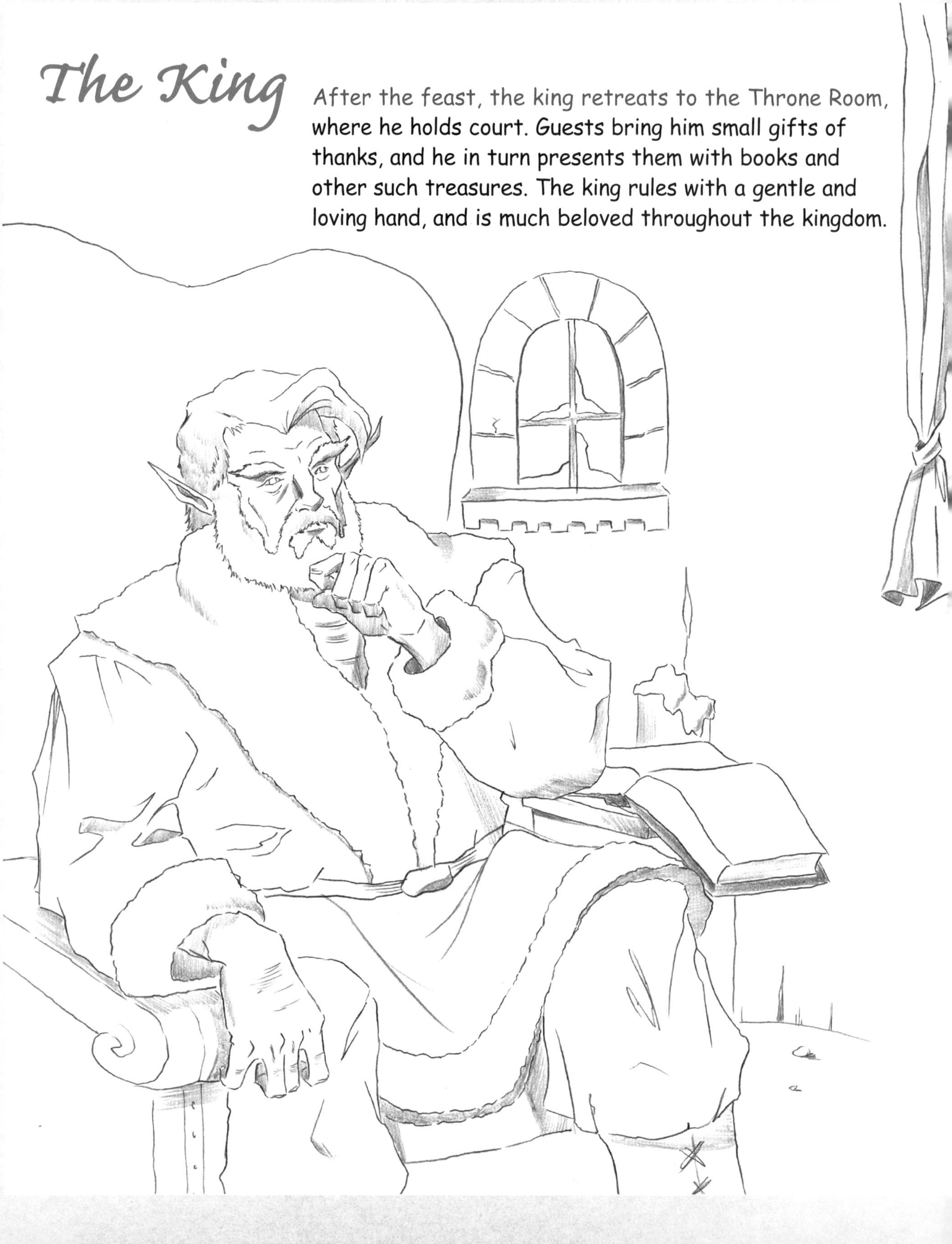

The Doctor

For those who sampled one too many treats at the feast, or even nine or ten too many, there is always the doctor. An experienced physician—who, by the way, requires no referral slips—he can fix an upset stomach in no time. Unfortunately, he can do little about an overindulgent appetite.

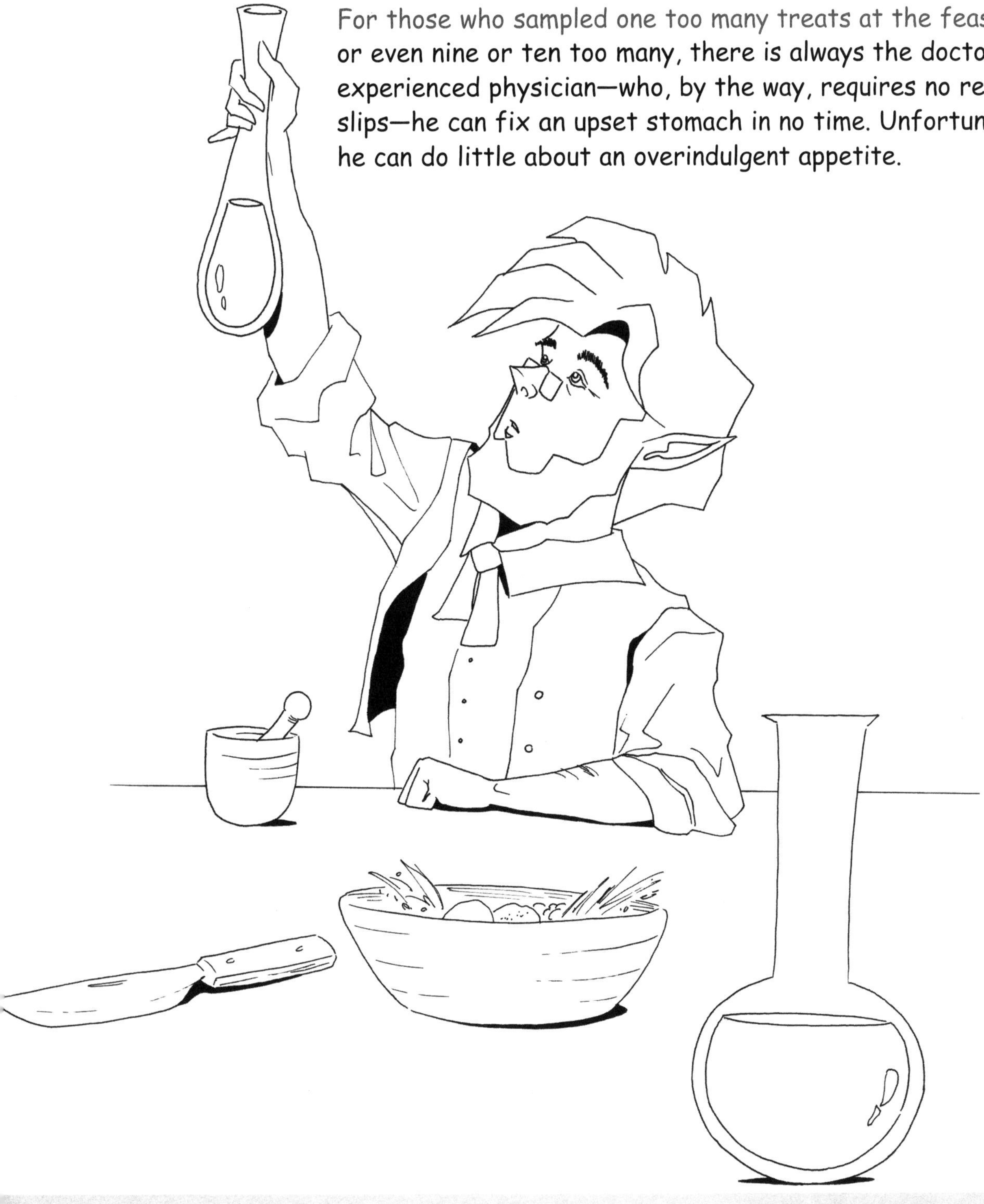

The Lawyer

I am truly not a fan of this old coot, always quoting from *The Great Book of Faerie.* I understand that rules are meaningless unless followed, but must every infraction be cause for penalties and fines?

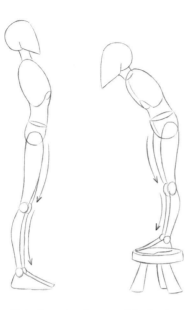

Note the natural curve of the leg bones, regardless of the size of the faerie.

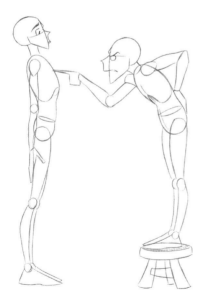

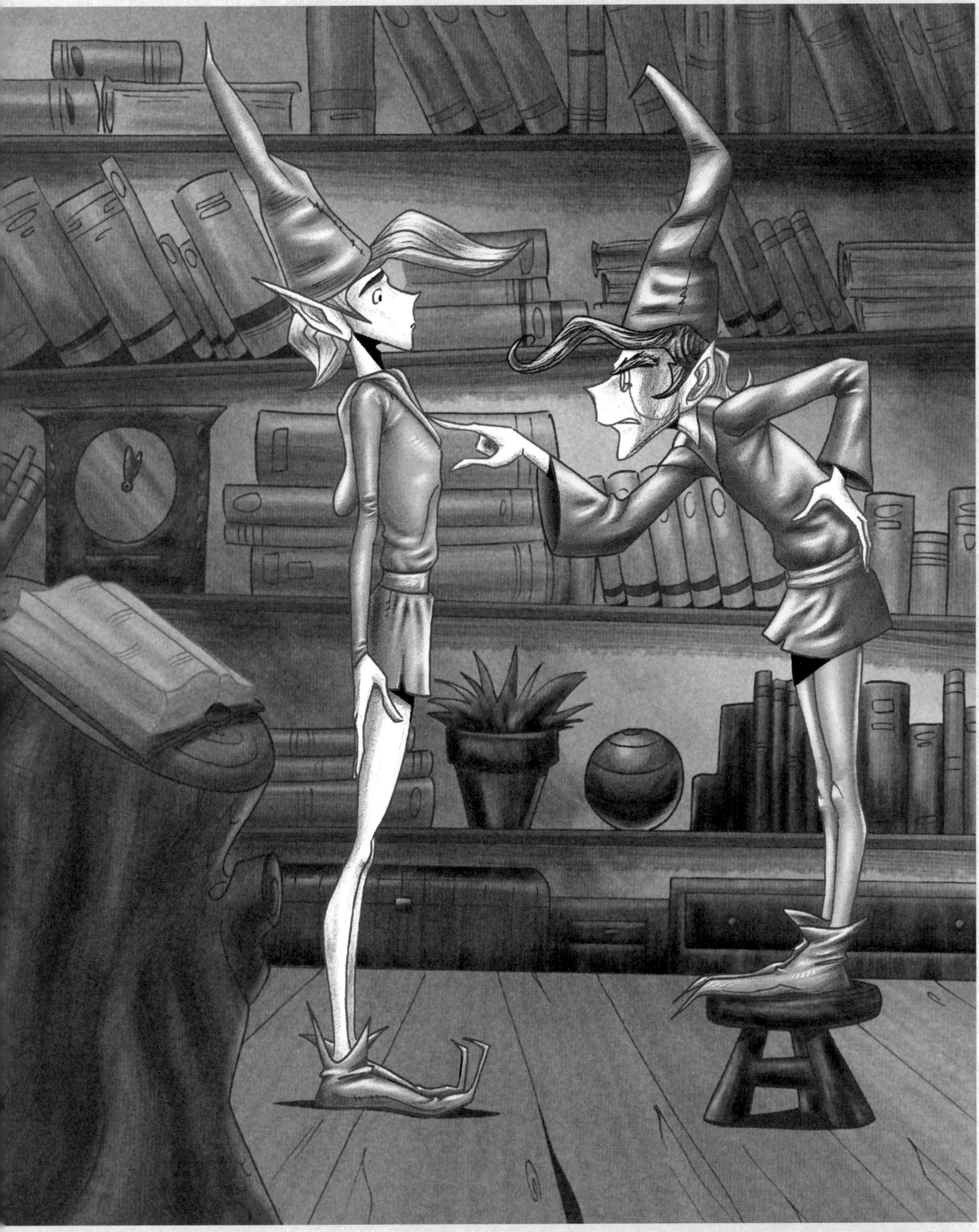

Friends and Foes

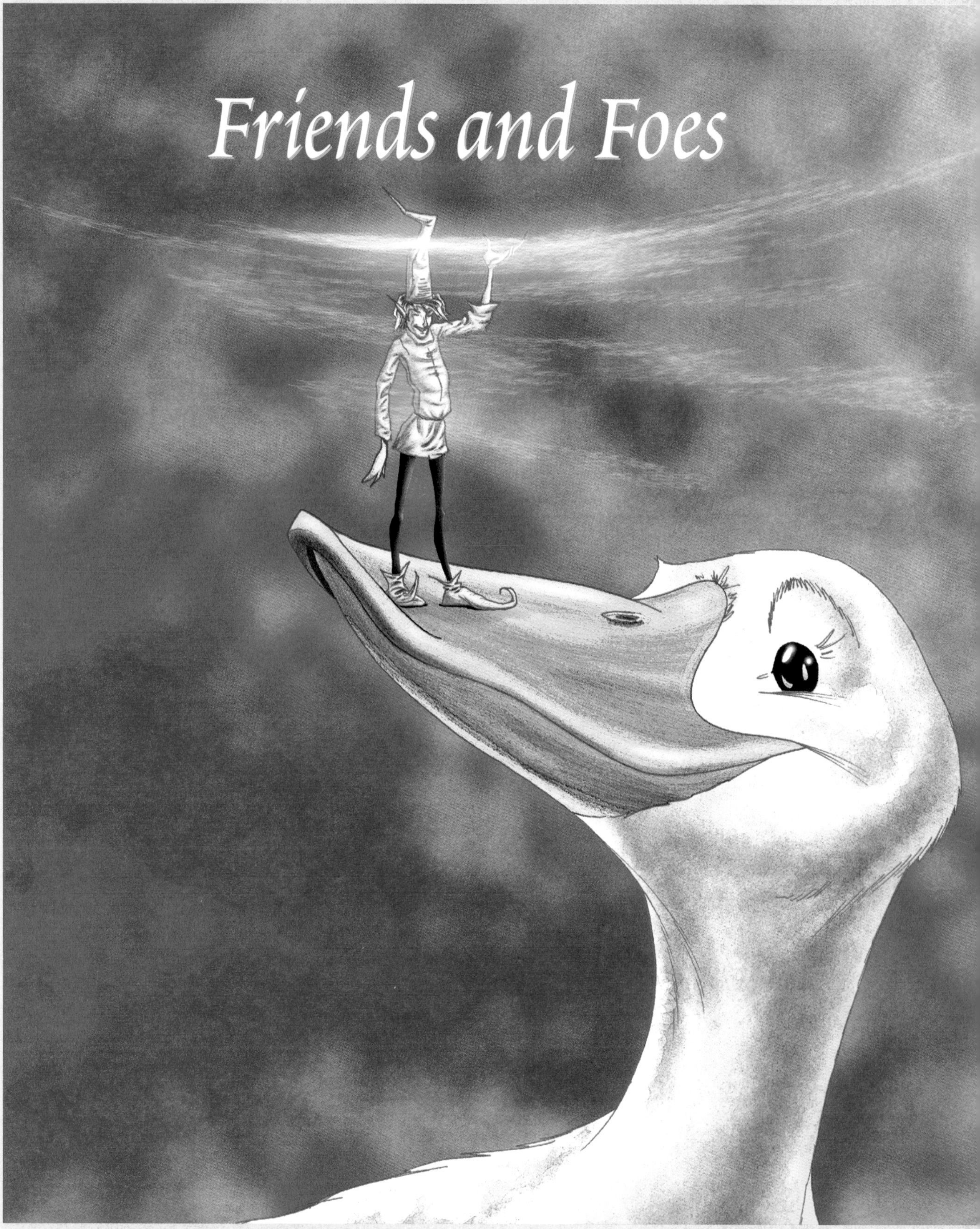

Special Pets

Dogs are good, aren't they? I've always believed that. But it wasn't until I saw one with a faerie that my feelings were completely confirmed. Canines seem to have an intuitive understanding of the vulnerability of faeries. They treat them with the care and protection they would afford one of their own puppies. And faeries just adore dogs, the furrier the better.

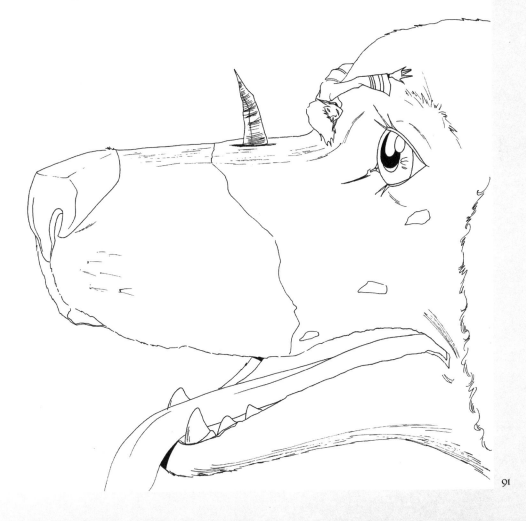

Honeybees

Honeybees, although usually aggressive in defending their hive, graciously allow certain faeries to partake of the honey. In return, the faeries alert the bees to the first patch of flowers blossoming in the spring.

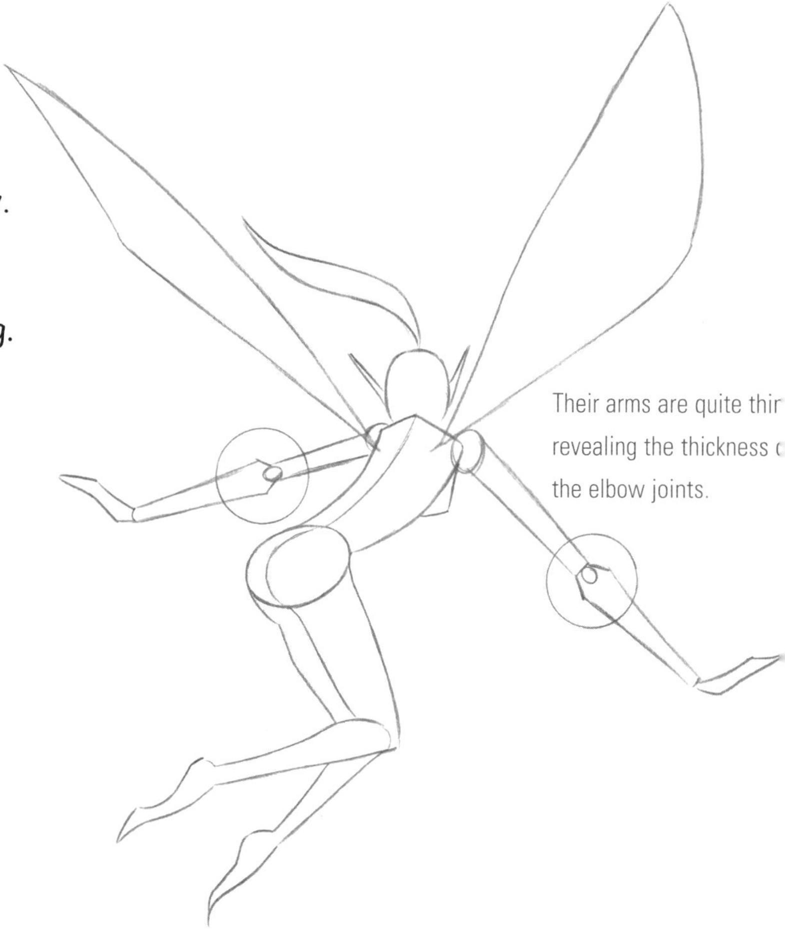

Their arms are quite thin, revealing the thickness of the elbow joints.

The line of the back obscures the bottom of the head.

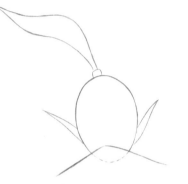

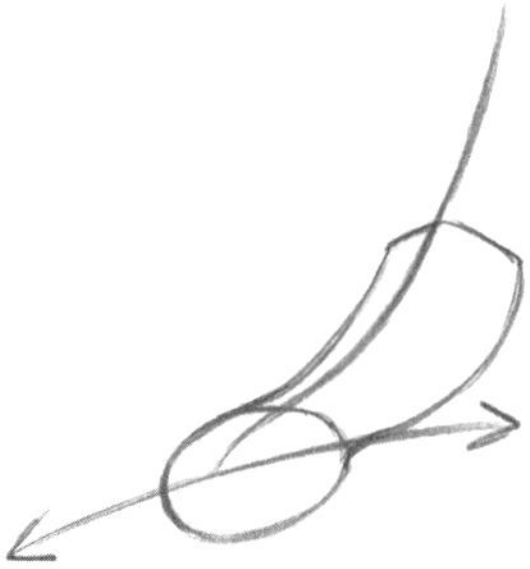

Note the diagonal angle at which the hips are drawn.

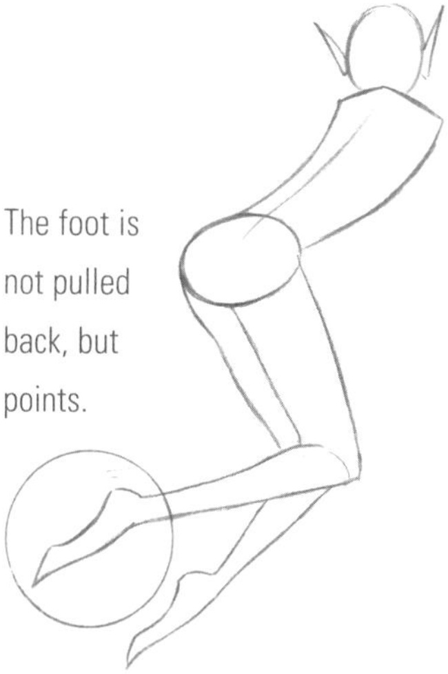

The foot is not pulled back, but points.

Note the curves of the fo

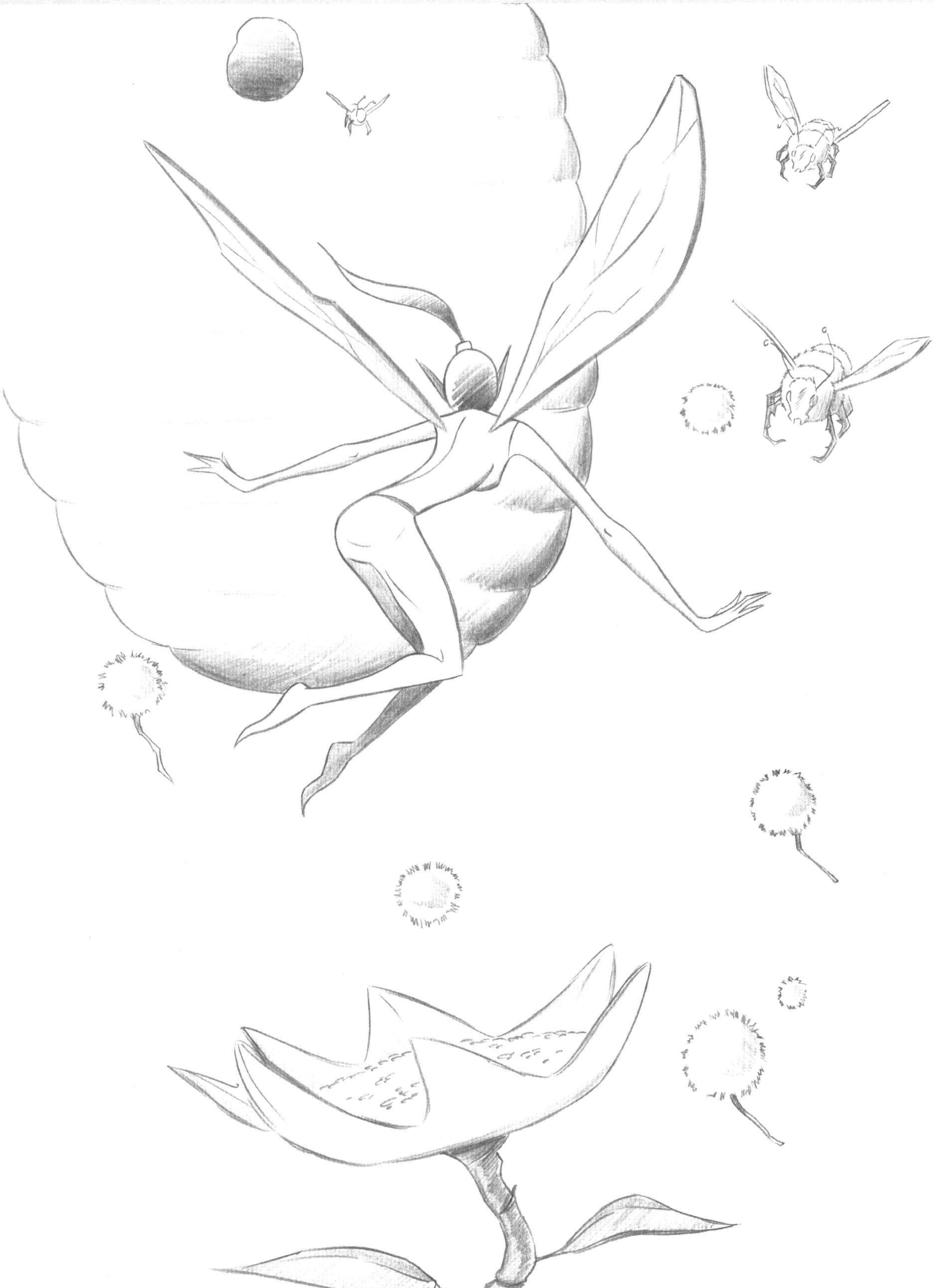

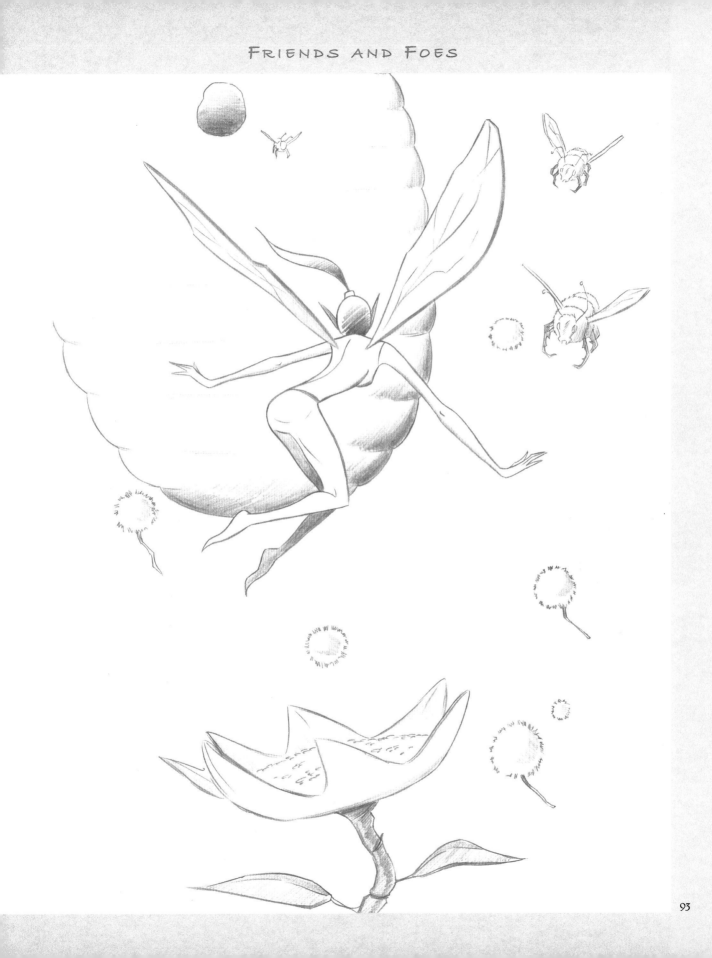

Caterpillars

Like dogs, some creatures will devote themselves utterly to you if you feed them and love them. I prefer pets with fur, but then again, I can't do this trick with my dog.

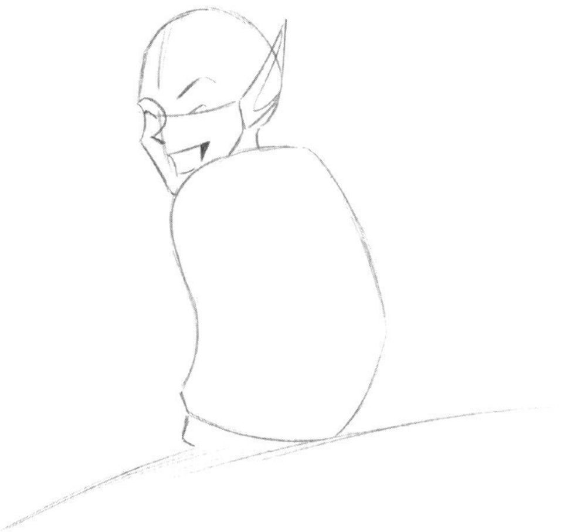

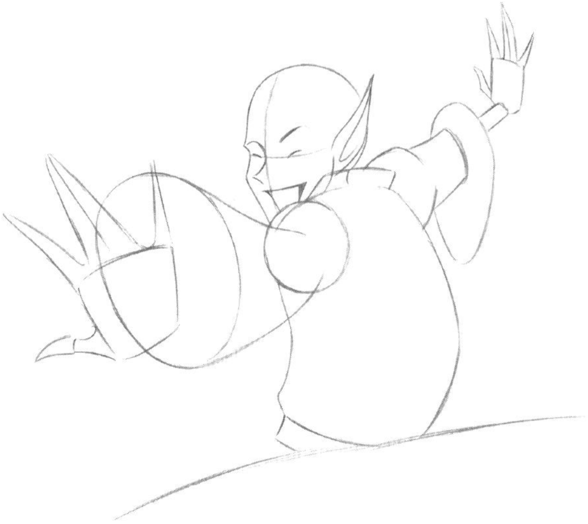

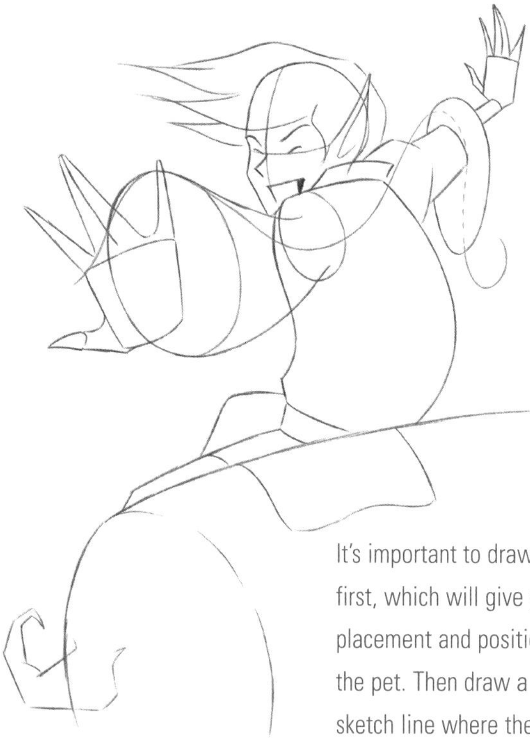

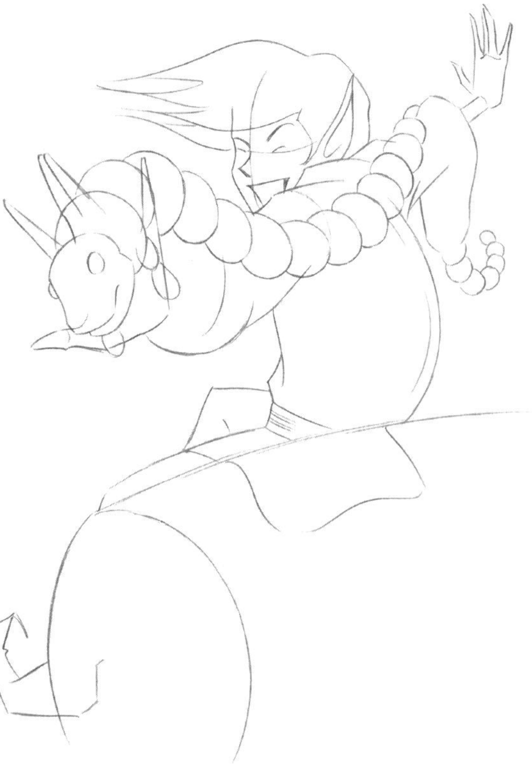

It's important to draw the faerie first, which will give you the placement and positioning for the pet. Then draw a simple sketch line where the pet will go, and construct the pet on top of it.

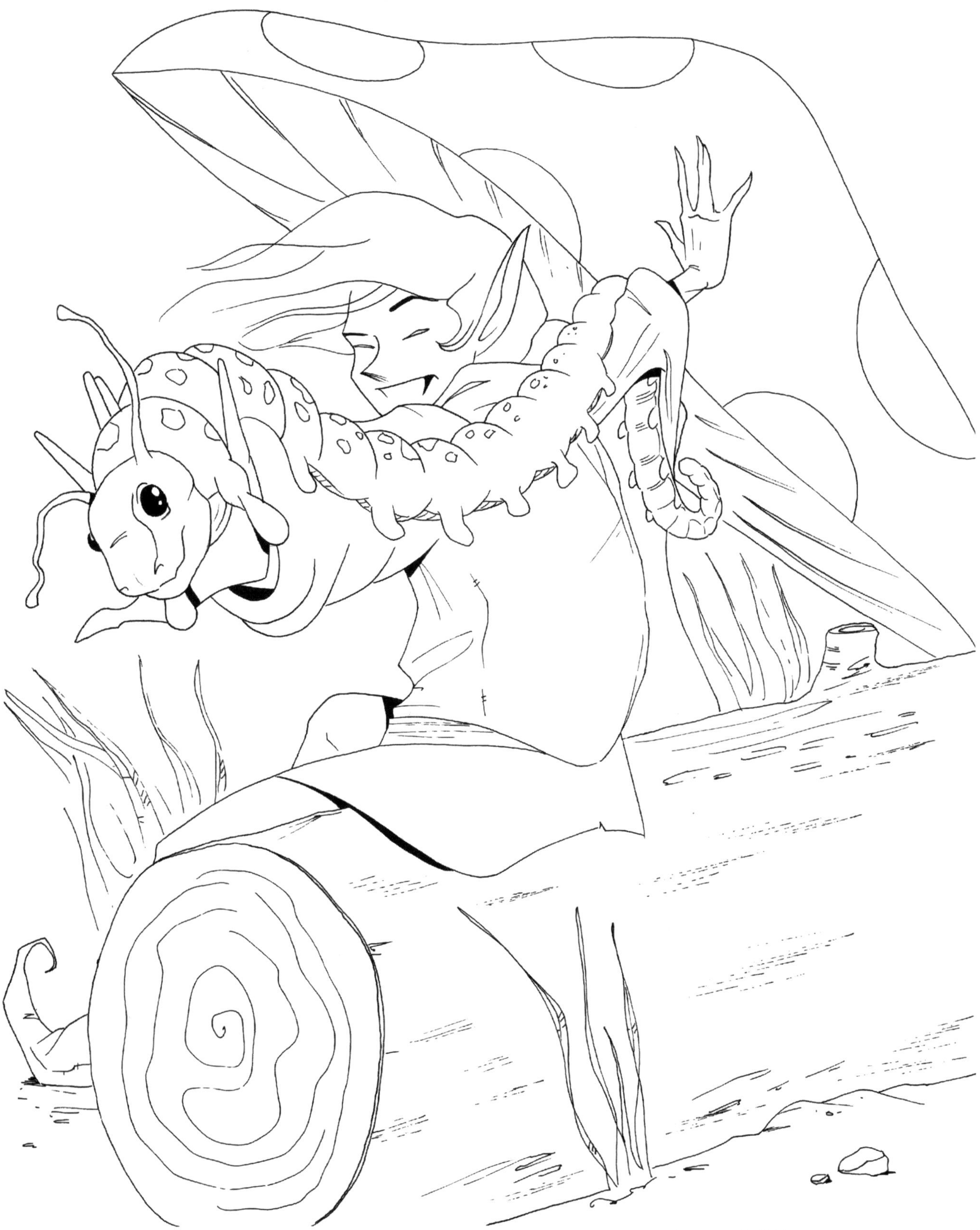

At the Races

The autumnal races are fun-filled, half-day events. Curiously, instead of awarding the prize to the winner of the race, faeries give it to the loser.

They figure that if the winner gets to win, then the loser should get something, too. I once tried to explain to them that the winner is supposed to

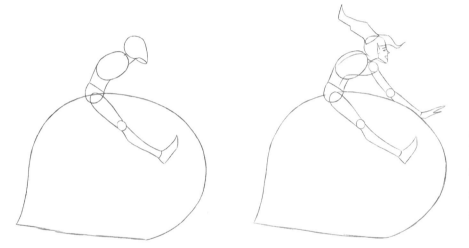

Snails are big (well, relatively speaking), peaceable creatures. Their shells are a series of concentric circles that are always stacked off center.

win everything. "Then what does the loser get?" they asked, certain that we humans wouldn't let someone go home feeling like a loser. "We...umm...usually throw the loser a party," I said. Okay, so I fibbed, but if you saw the looks on their faces, you'd understand.

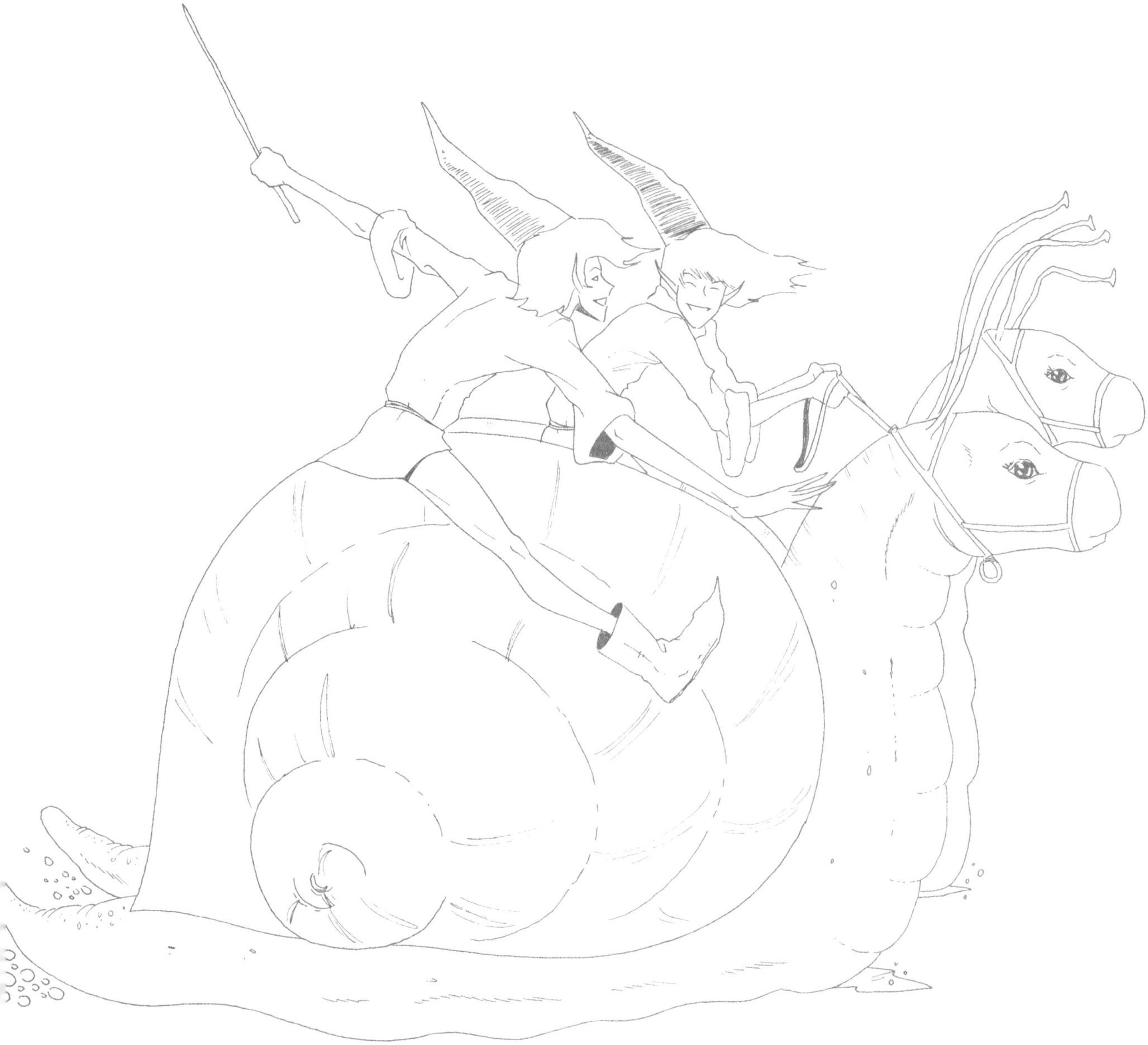

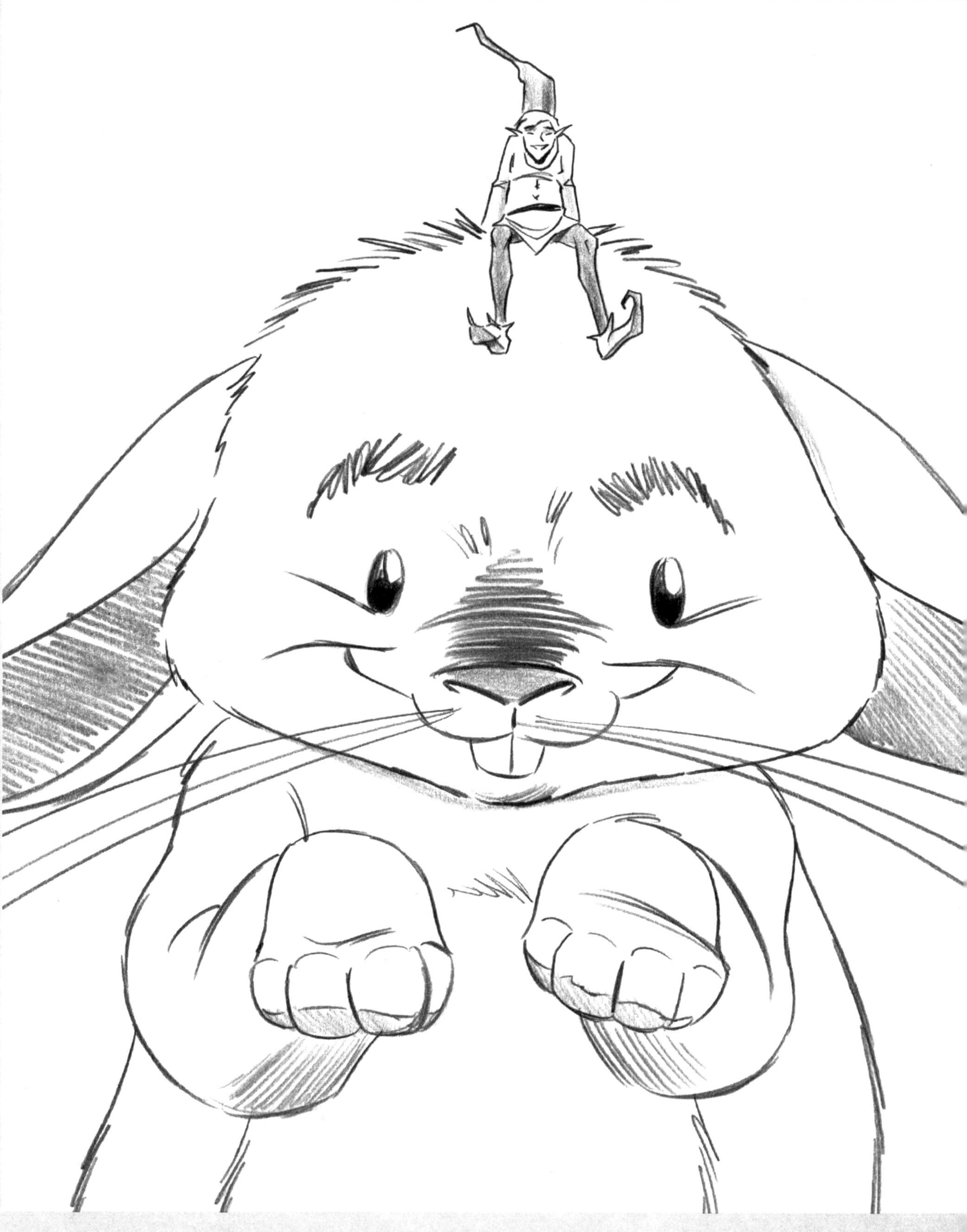

The Trouble with Bunnies

No, no, don't get me wrong: bunnies are fond of faeries. But, bunnies are apt to suddenly hop and leap without notice or thought to who may be astride them. Nonetheless, some faeries find them irresistible.

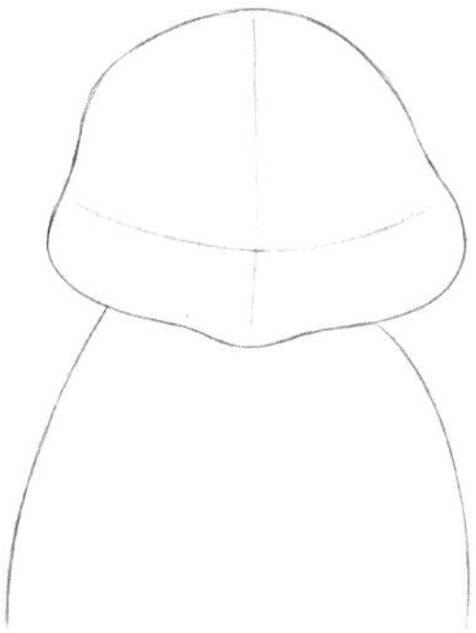

The top of the bunny's head is a favorite seat. With every turn, the faerie gets a magnificent view of the kingdom.

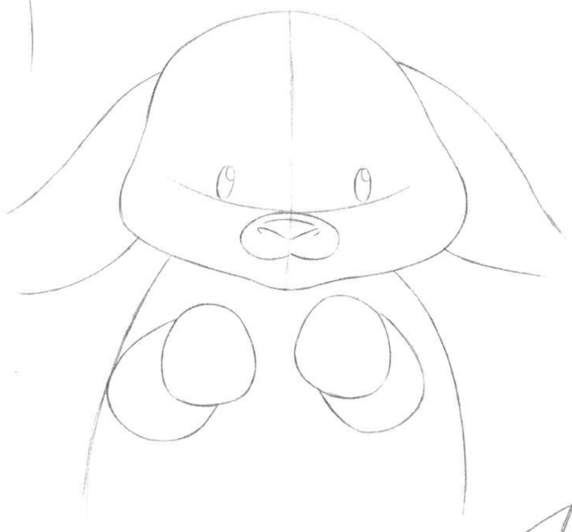

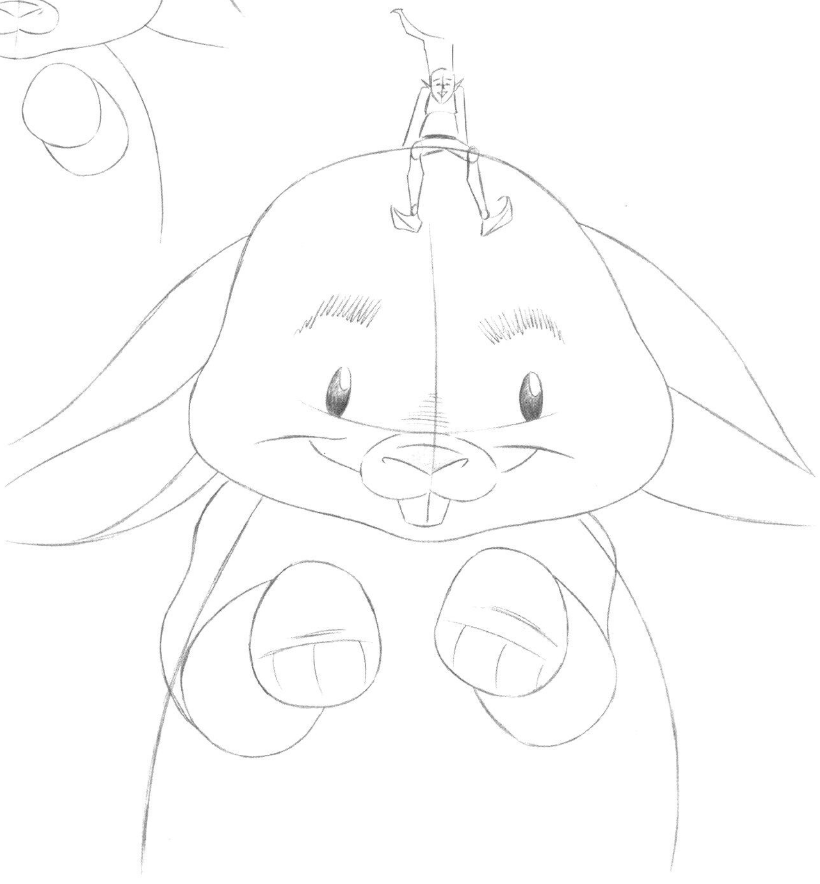

Evil Enemies

Despite their gentle and good nature, faeries do have a few enemies. Aside from avoiding animals, like cats, that may perceive the tiny beings as prey, faeries must protect themselves from wicked beings that try to channel faerie magic in order to damage nearby villages and cast evil spells.

The Conjurer

Looked at askance by the villagers, the Master Conjurer studies from the *Minor Book of Charms and Incantations,* which is one of the later books of faerie and not recognized by the King.

He has quite a severe face. Behind those piercing eyes is a wealth of knowledge and wisdom, although he has been known to apply his shrewdness to traitorous practices.

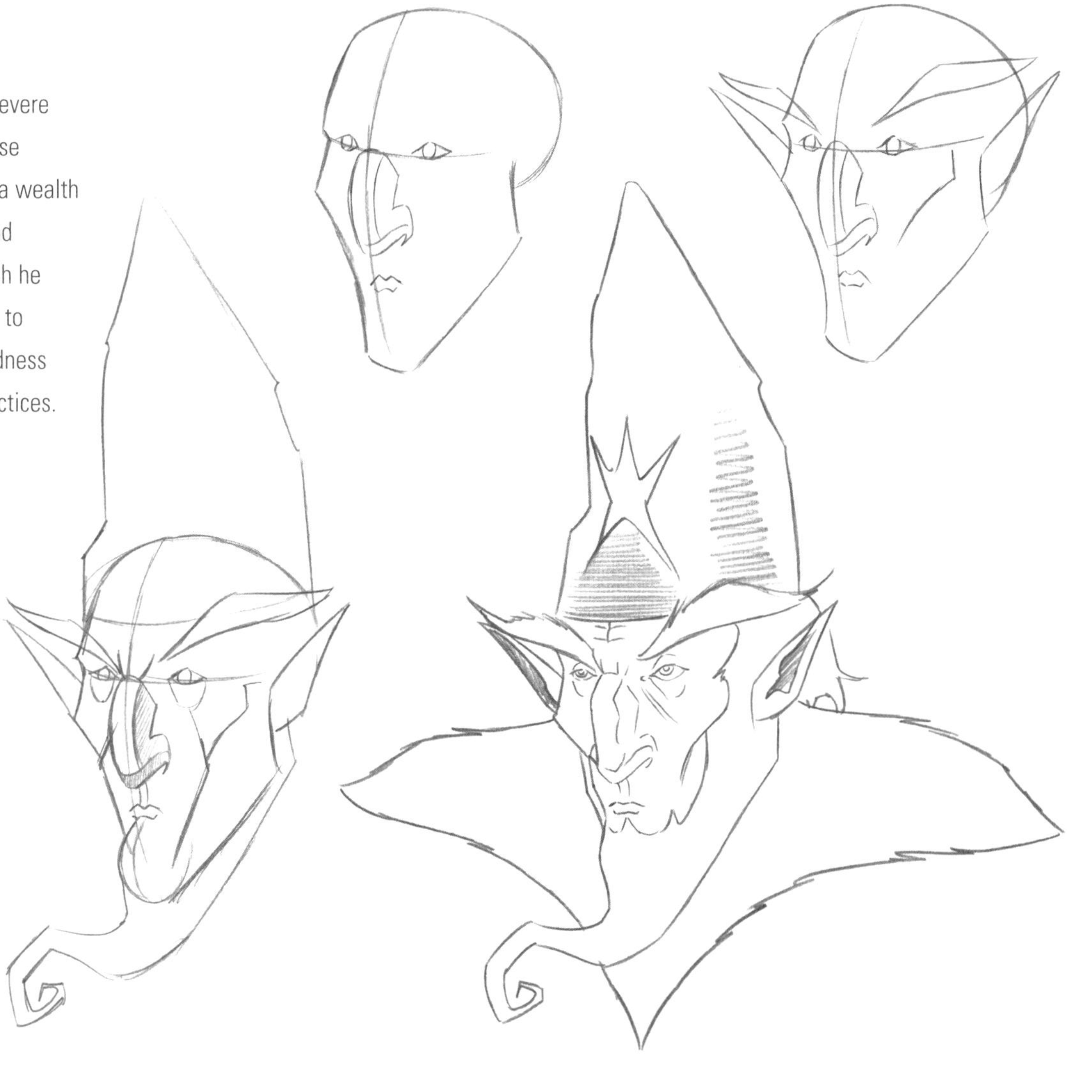

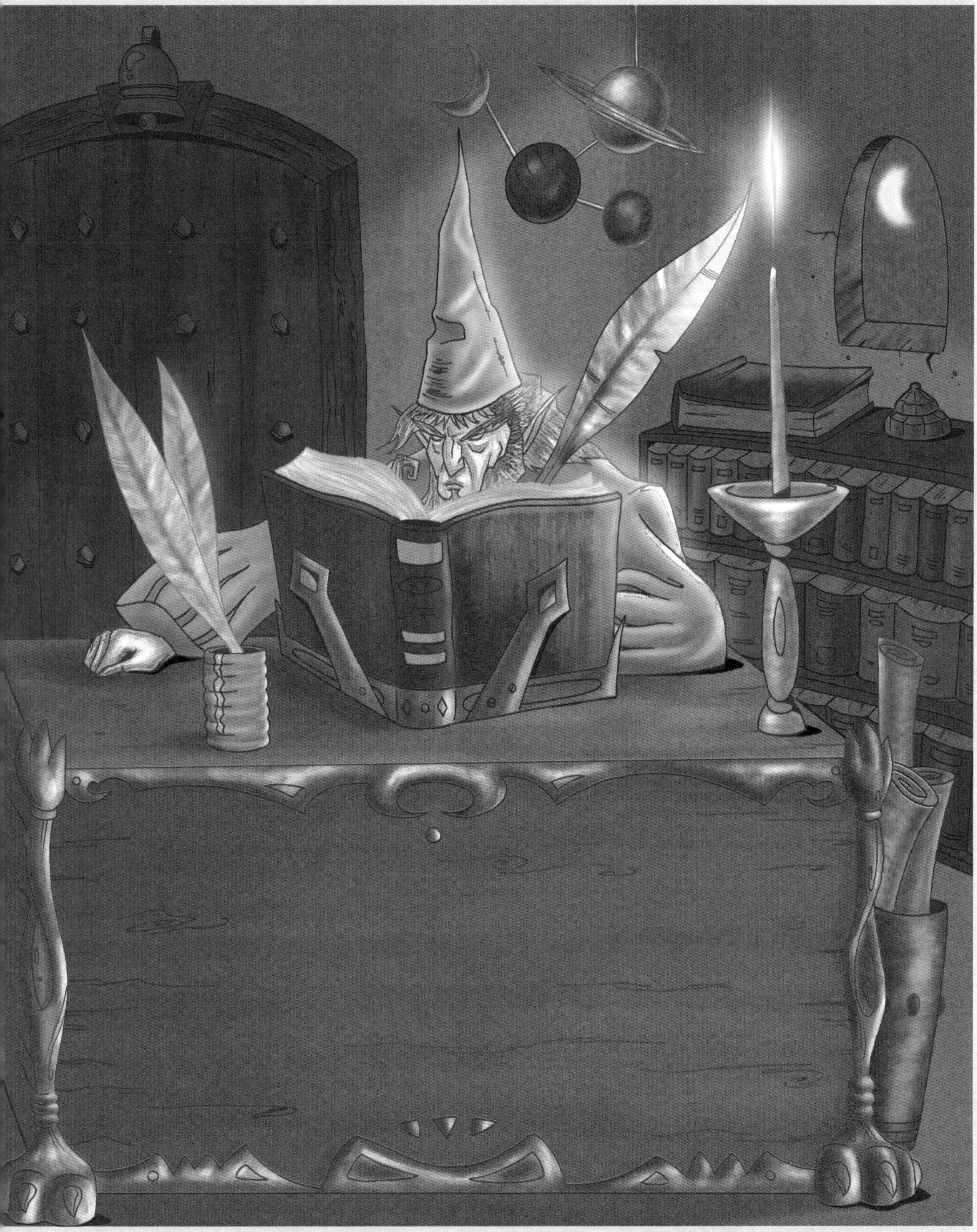

Once a faerie has been judged by his peers as guilty of a treacherous act, the great walls of Noroon immediately rise above and draw around him—and he is banished.

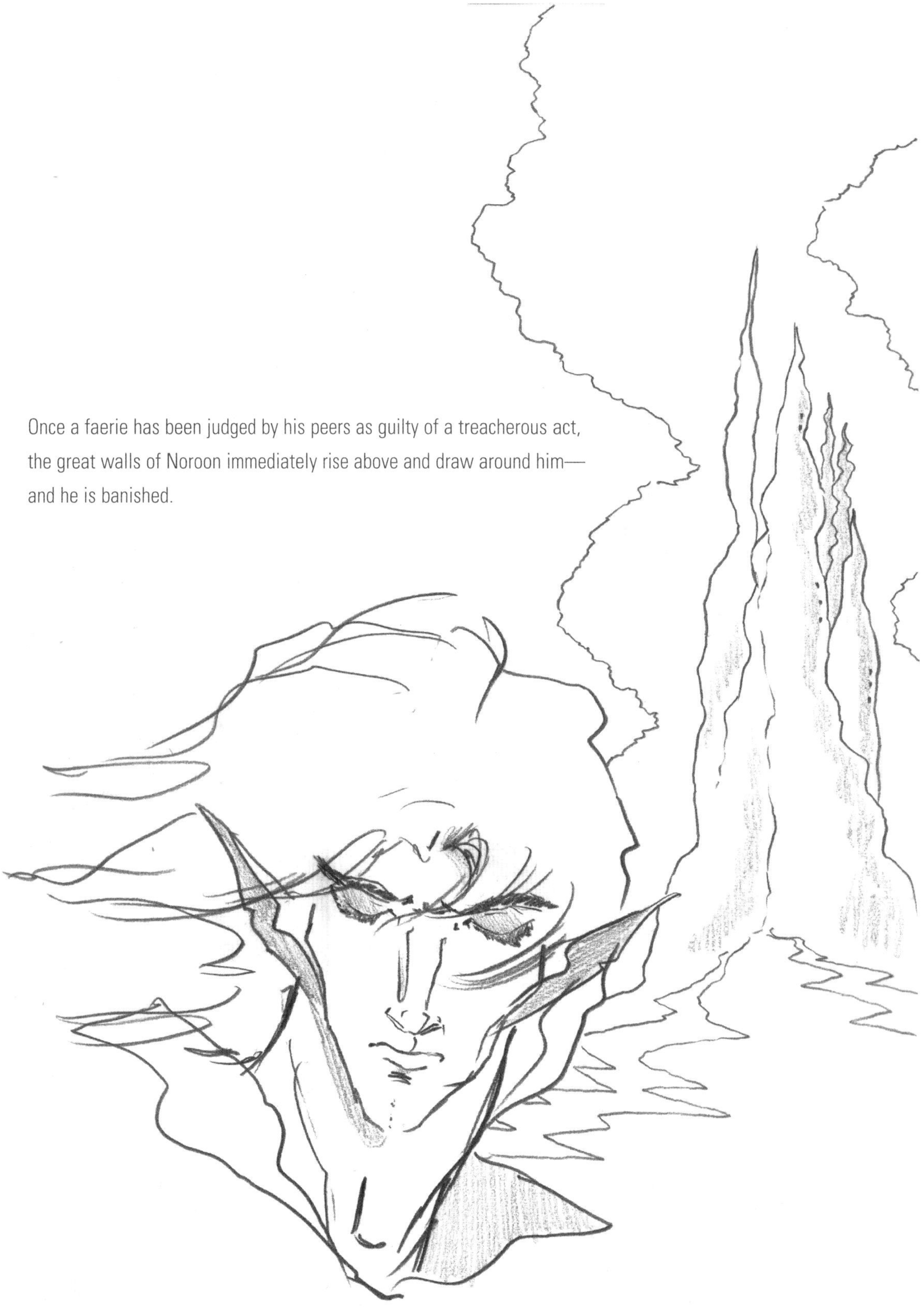

Banishment

The worst of all fates for faeries is to be banished to the land of Noroon. Once you enter this desolate land, you can never return. Although it may be theoretically *possible,* no one has done it, because it changes a faerie both physically and spiritually so that he or she no longer cares about the light, but craves the darkness. Only one act warrants this ultimate penalty: the practice of the dark arts.

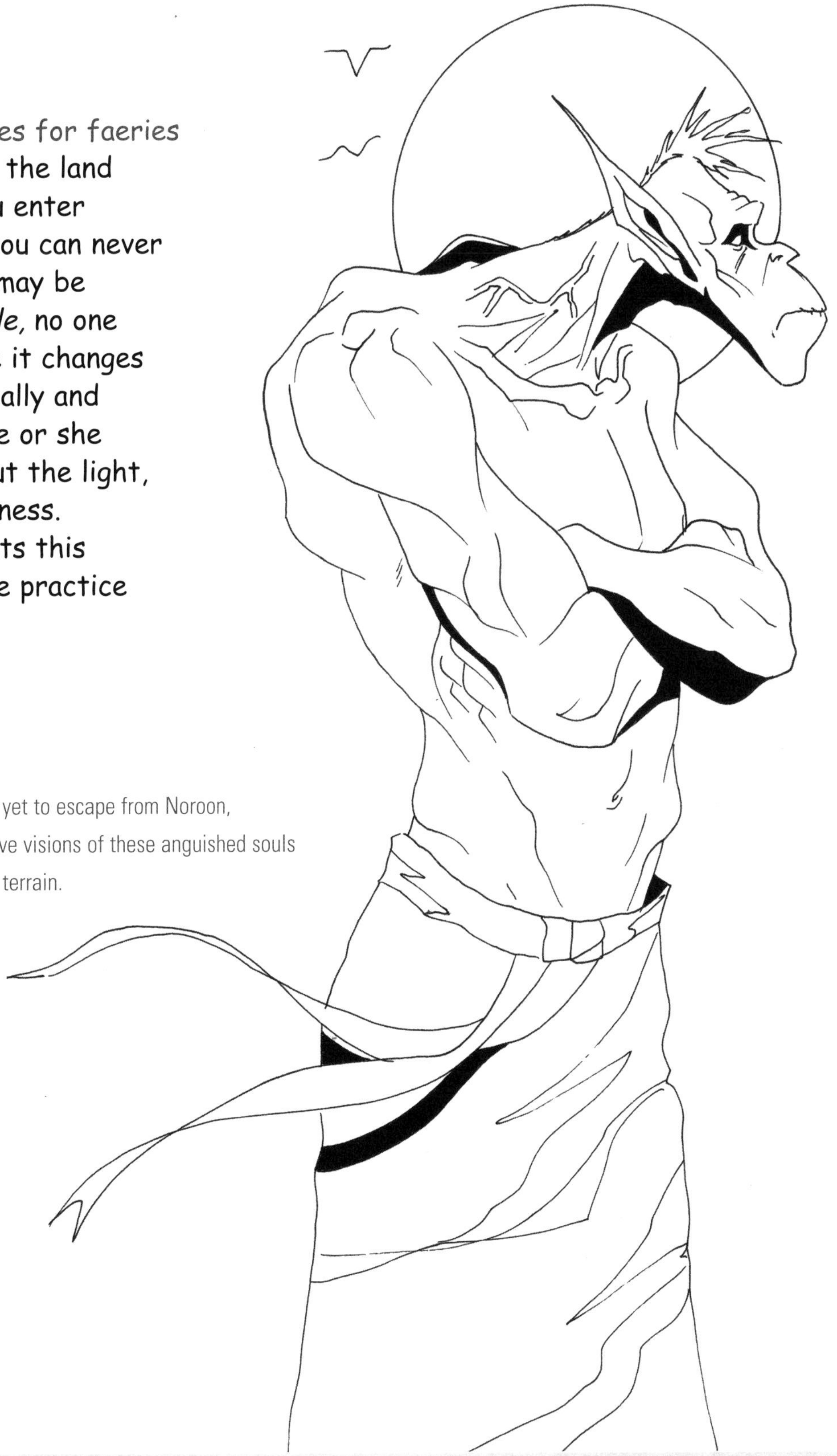

While a condemned faerie has yet to escape from Noroon, dreamers have been said to have visions of these anguished souls roaming the dark and deserted terrain.

Charmed Creatures

Faeries inhabit a magical world teeming with spirits who travel through nature's hidden corridors. These charmed beings are generally friendly, but they are also shy and desirous of returning home, and often quickly vanish from whence they came.

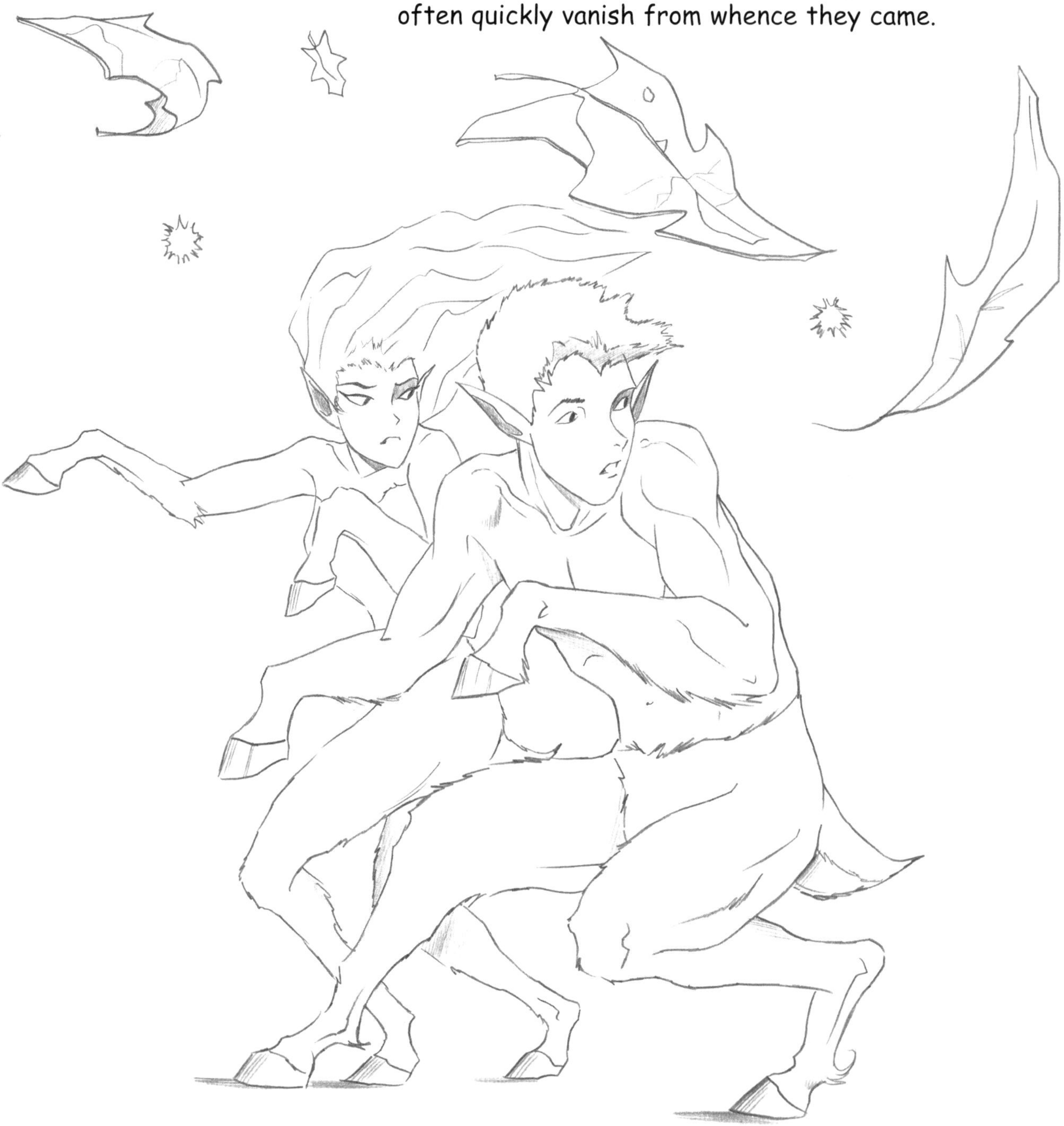

A Spirit Who Decided to Stay

G'Nock, a half-conjured horse, became quite a celebrity in the faerie kingdom. Being quite partial to himself in any event, he decided that he could get more attention if he stood out, than if he went back through the corridor and blended in…so he stayed. And it's been all for the good.

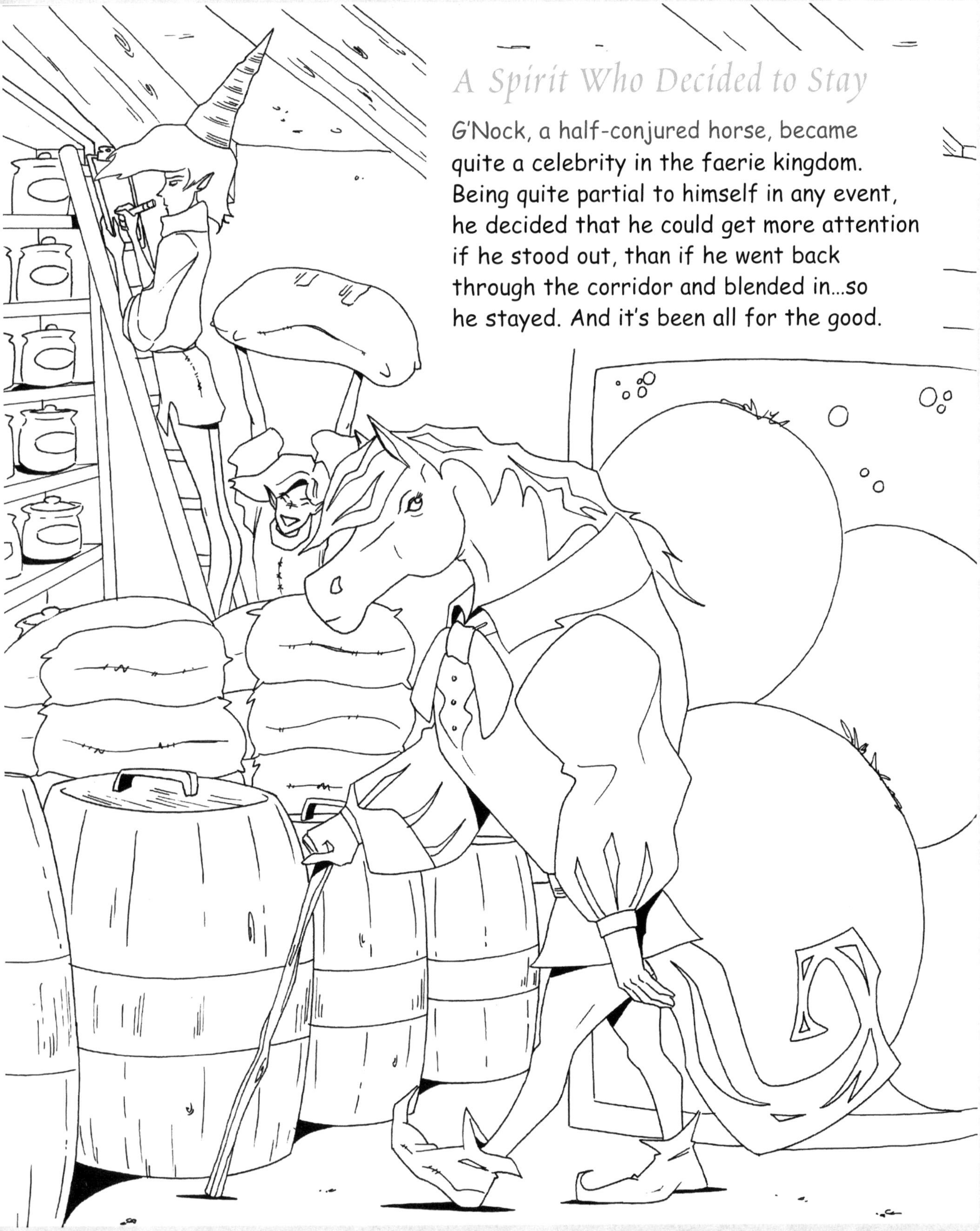

Mini Faeries

It may surprise you to learn that there are enchanted beings even smaller than faeries. Because of the tremendous difference in size, neither I nor any human to my knowledge has ever interacted with them. I have only glanced them briefly. Faeries seem to have a cordial relationship with them.

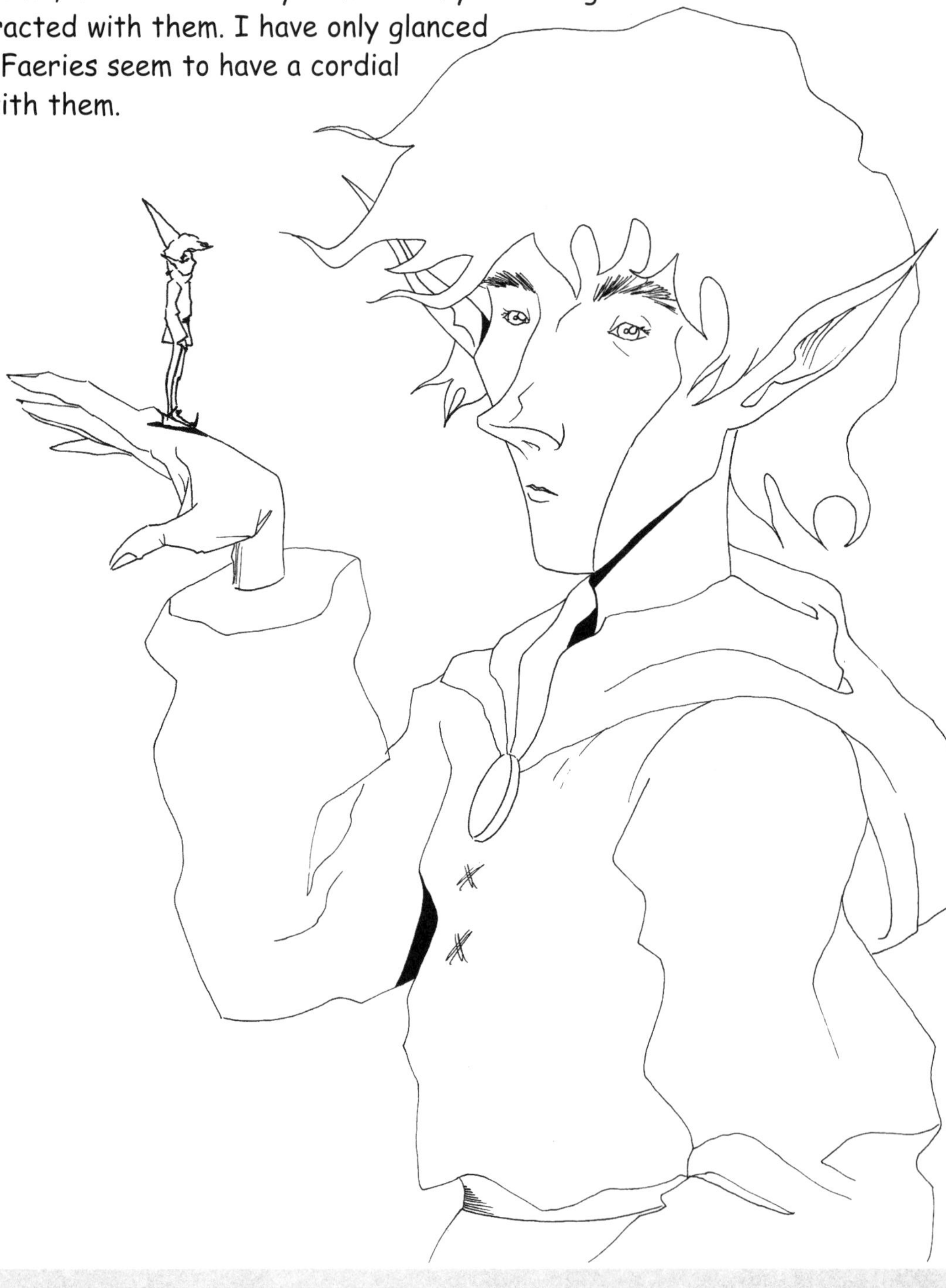

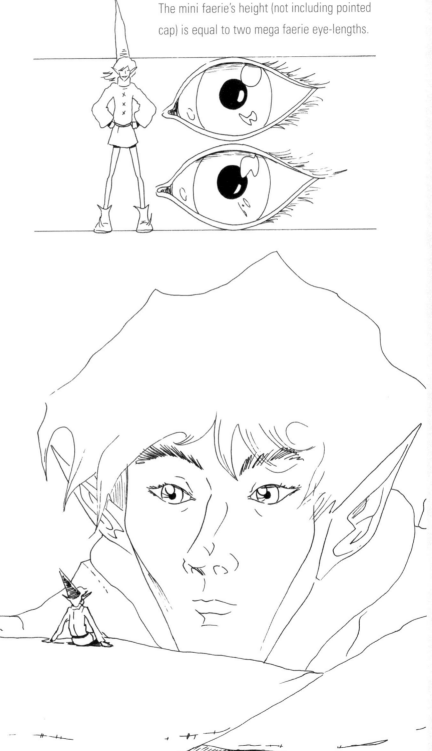

The mini faerie's height (not including pointed cap) is equal to two mega faerie eye-lengths.

I confess that I have guessed at the features and expressions of the mini faeries, as I haven't the eye power to clearly see a being quite so small. However, I can approximate their size. They are two eye-lengths tall, if measured against the eyes of a normal-sized faerie. Mini faeries wear tall hats, which I can just about make out from the pointed tip. There may be faeries even smaller than these, but I suspect that that is something we shall never know.

I do wonder which one is curiouser of the other—the big one or the small one.

Faces in the Clouds

I first noticed these wondrous spirits when I was still young, and Rollo and I ventured together deep into the woods. We had been running and laughing, far past the known fields and meadows. I remember being exhausted and falling, collapsing on my back to rest. "Where are we, Rollo?" I asked. "Are we lost?"

Rollo looked up. I thought he was getting his bearings. I happened to look at the same spot at that very moment, and I believe—no, I know—that I saw them, just for an instant, before they noticed me. Rollo darted ahead, and I sprang up to follow him. "We're not lost," he replied. But he had been. I know it.

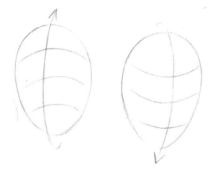

When an object tilts *downward* the guidelines arc *upward*, across the surface.

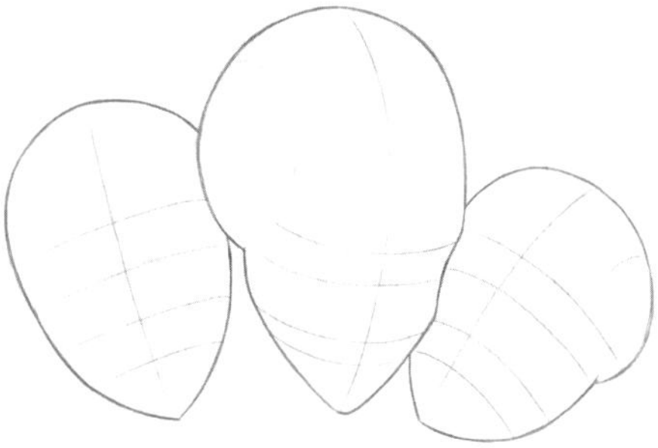

When an object tilts *upward*, the guidelines arc *downward* across the surface.

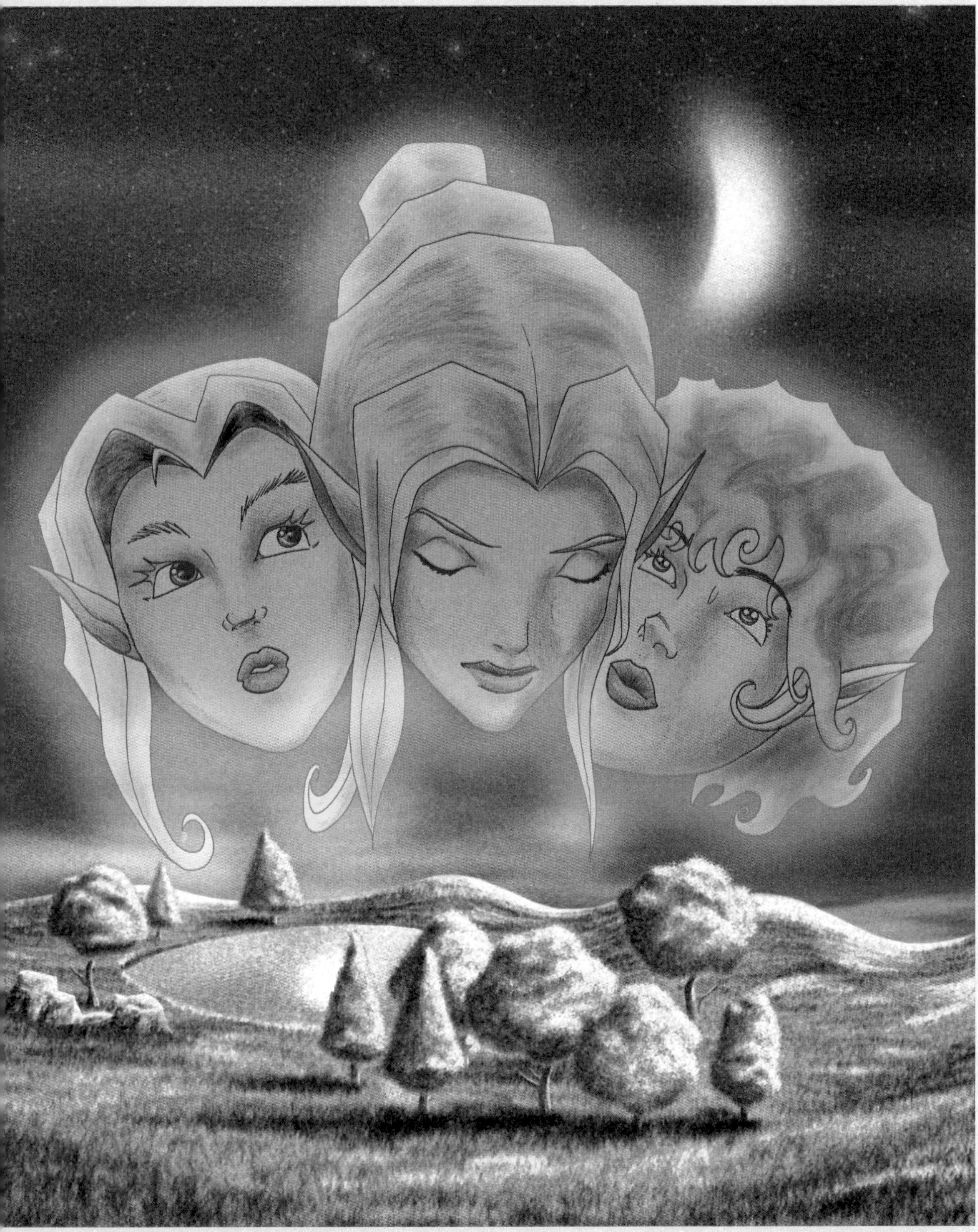

The legends of faeries don't always chronicle courageous warriors, like the one below, who defend the land from evil and treachery. However, the kingdom could not have survived without them. But that's the subject of another book.

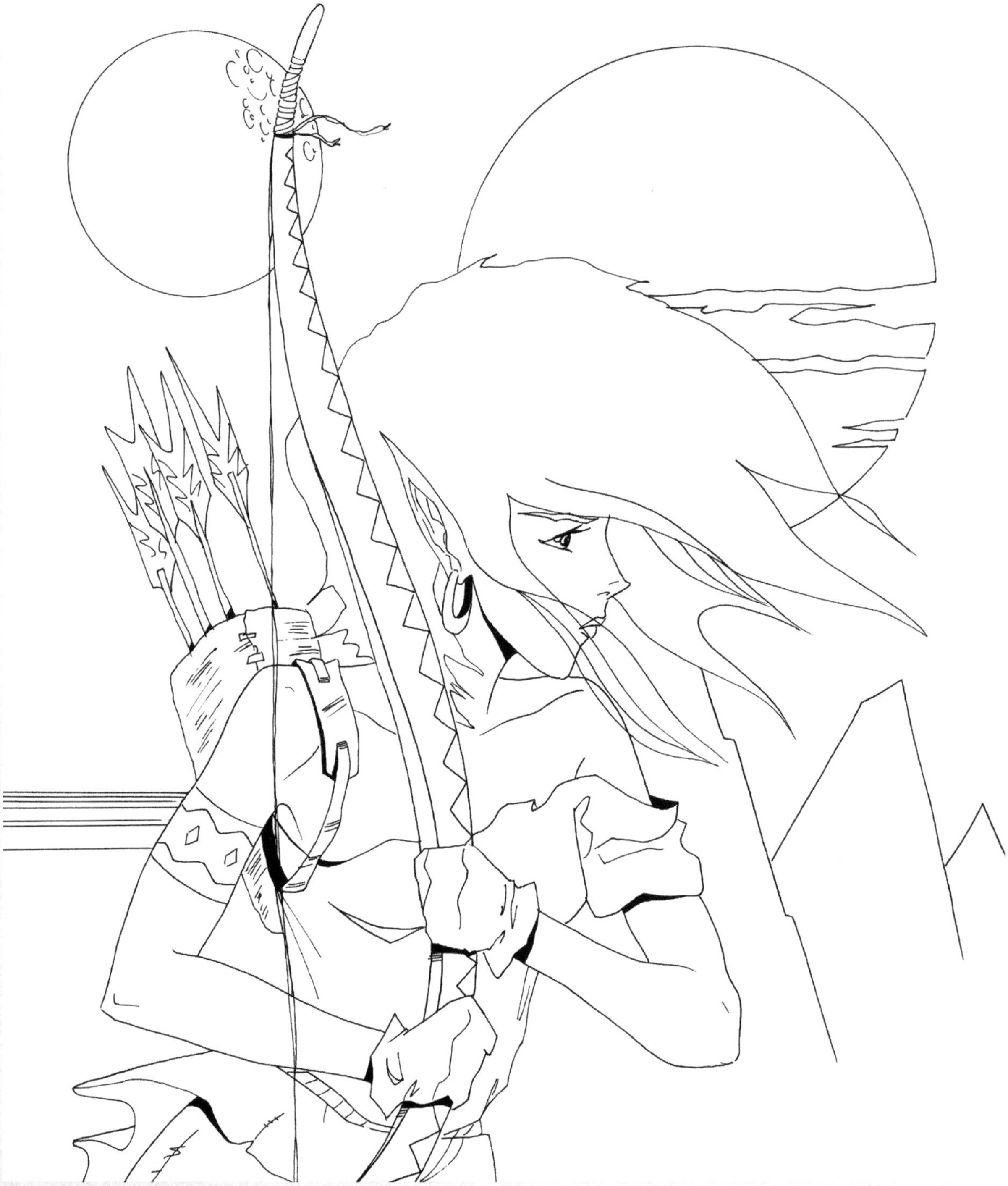

And so this journal has come to an end. But your journey with the faeries is, I suspect, just beginning. You may not know where my secret green meadow lies, and I may not know yours—yet, I imagine each of us has a special spot where our hearts and minds do roam.

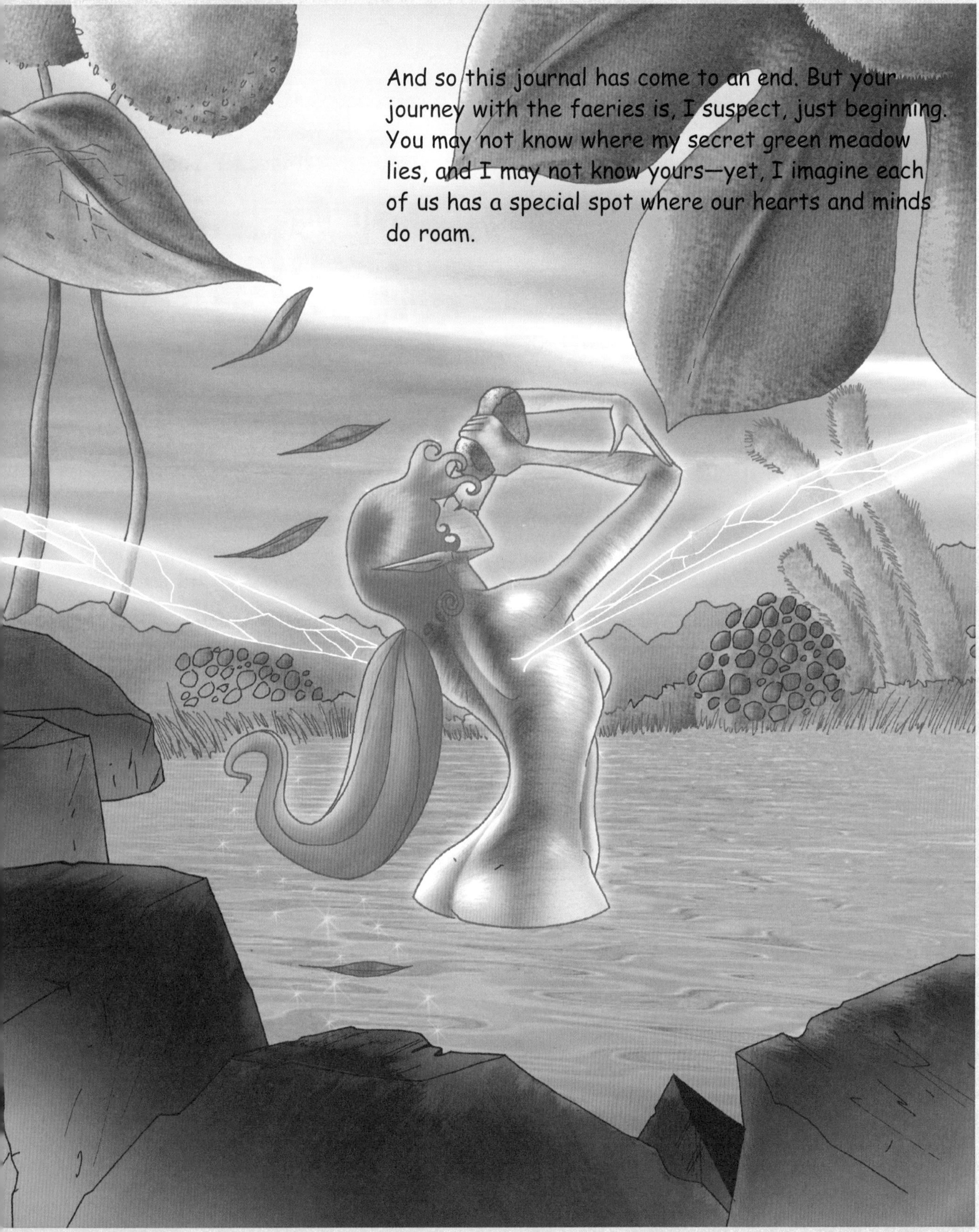

My sincere thanks to Candace Raney for shepherding this book and bringing it to fruition, and to Anne McNamara for her care and her thoughtful editing. Thanks to Bob Ferro, Sharon Kaplan, Charles Whang, Ellen Greene, Alisa Palazzo, and Lee Wiggins of Watson-Guptill; and Stan, Frank, and John at MADA Design.